Pastoral Care
for Post-Traumatic Stress
Disorder
Healing the Shattered Soul

THE HAWORTH PASTORAL PRESS
Religion and Mental Health
Harold G. Koenig, MD
Senior Editor

New, Recent, and Forthcoming Titles:

Adventures in Senior Living: Learning How to Make Retirement Meaningful and Enjoyable by J. Lawrence Driskill

Dying, Grieving, Faith, and Family: A Pastoral Care Approach by George W. Bowman

The Pastoral Care of Depression: A Guidebook by Binford W. Gilbert

Understanding Clergy Misconduct in Religious Systems: Scapegoating, Family Secrets, and the Abuse of Power by Candace R. Benyei

What the Dying Teach Us: Lessons on Living by Samuel Lee Oliver

The Pastor's Family: The Challenges of Family Life and Pastoral Responsibilities by Daniel L. Langford

Somebody's Knocking at Your Door: AIDS and the African-American Church by Ronald Jeffrey Weatherford and Carole Boston Weatherford

Grief Education for Caregivers of the Elderly by Junietta Baker McCall

The Obsessive-Compulsive Disorder: Pastoral Care for the Road to Change by Robert M. Collie

The Pastoral Care of Children by David H. Grossoehme

Ways of the Desert: Becoming Holy Through Difficult Times by William F. Kraft

Caring for a Loved One with Alzheimer's Disease: A Christian Perspective by Elizabeth T. Hall

"Martha, Martha": How Christians Worry by Elaine Leong Eng

Spiritual Care for Children Living in Specialized Settings: Breathing Underwater by Michael F. Friesen

Broken Bodies, Healing Hearts: Reflections of a Hospital Chaplain by Gretchen W. TenBrook

Shared Grace: Therapists and Clergy Working Together by Marion Bilich, Susan Bonfiglio, and Steven Carlson

The Pastor's Guide to Psychiatric Disorders and Mental Health Resources by W. Brad Johnson and William L. Johnson

Pastoral Counseling: A Gestalt Approach by Ward A. Knights

Christ-Centered Therapy: Empowering the Self by Russ Harris

Bioethics from a Faith Perspective: Ethics in Health Care for the Twenty-First Century by Jack Hanford

Family Abuse and the Bible: The Scriptural Perspective by Aimee K. Cassiday-Shaw

When the Caregiver Becomes the Patient: A Journey from a Mental Disorder to Recovery and Compassionate Insight by Daniel L. Langford and Emil J. Authelet

A Theology of God-Talk: The Language of the Heart by J. Timothy Allen

A Practical Guide to Hospital Ministry: Healing Ways by Junietta B. McCall

Pastoral Care for Post-Traumatic Stress Disorder: Healing the Shattered Soul by Daléne Fuller Rogers

Integrating Spirit and Psyche: Using Women's Narratives in Psychotherapy by Mary Pat Henehan

Chronic Pain: Biomedical and Spiritual Approaches by Harold G. Koenig

Pastoral Care
for Post-Traumatic Stress
Disorder
Healing the Shattered Soul

Daléne C. Fuller Rogers, MDiv

Routledge
Taylor & Francis Group
New York   London

Routledge is an imprint of the
Taylor & Francis Group, an informa business

Reprinted 2009 by Routledge

Excerpts reprinted with the permission of Simon & Schuster from THE NEW OUR BODIES OURSELVES by The Boston Women's Health Book Collective. Copyright © 1984, 1992 by The Boston Women's Health Book Collective.

Cover design by Jennifer M. Gaska.

Library of Congress Cataloging-in-Publication Data

Rogers, Daléne Fuller.
    Pastoral care for post-traumatic stress disorder : healing the shattered soul / Daléne Fuller Rogers.
        p. cm.
    Includes bibliographical references and index.
    ISBN 0-7890-1541-2 (alk. paper) — ISBN 0-7890-1542-0 (alk. paper)
    1. Post-traumatic stress disorder—Patients—Pastoral counseling of. I. Title.

RC552.P67 R6436 2002
616.85'21—dc21
                                                             2001051685

To the women, children, and men who have died from traumatic incidents, and to those who have survived trauma and tenaciously struggled to be healed in body, mind, and spirit.

ABOUT THE AUTHOR

Reverend Daléne C. Fuller Rogers, MDiv, BCETS, was ordained by the Anglican Church of Canada in 1990 and now ministers with the United Church of Christ. She is a diplomate of the American Academy of Experts in Traumatic Stress, a professional chaplain in the National Association of Veterans Administration Chaplains (NAVAC), and a member of the Military Chaplains Association and the Association of Conflict Resolution.

In more than a decade of ordained ministry, Reverend Fuller Rogers has devoted much of her time to working with women survivors of domestic and sexual violence. She served on the Board of Directors of the Kitchener-Waterloo Sexual Assault Support Center (Waterloo, Ontario) and acted as chaplain to the volunteer staff. She was a nominee for Kitchener-Waterloo Woman of the Year in the humanitarian category in 1991. During her time in Canada, she organized an ecumenical healing service in memory of the women murdered in December, 1998, at the L'Ecole Polytechnologie in Montreal. In 1992, she was the chaplain and seminar leader for the Diocese of Huron, Ontario, Canada's three-part series, "Childhood Sexual Abuse: The Church's Response."

Reverend Fuller Rogers was an advisor to the Episcopal Diocese of Vermont in the formulation of their clergy abuse prevention guidelines and has been an annual speaker and advisor to the SOS peer counselors group at Woodstock Union High School (Woodstock, Vermont) since 1994. In 1997, she joined the chaplaincy staff of the Veteran's Healthcare Administration Hospital in White River Junction, Vermont, the location of the National Center for PTSD.

CONTENTS

Foreword   **ix**
   Lawrence L. LaPierre

Acknowledgments   **xiii**

**Chapter 1. Defining Post-Traumatic Stress Disorder
   and Its Causes**   **1**

   Sexual Trauma   3
   Physical Trauma   5
   Psychological Trauma   7
   Spiritual Trauma   8
   Eyewitnesses and Survivors of Disaster   10

Chapter 2. Symptoms of PTSD   **13**

Chapter 3. Common Manifestations   **17**

   Spiritual Issues: Grief and Anger   18

Chapter 4. Psychological Complications   **25**

   Church As Redemptive Community   28

Chapter 5. Theological Dimensions of Spiritual Trauma   **31**

   Theodicy and Suffering   31
   Spiritual Care and Healing   35
   Forgiveness   38
   Prayer, Meditation, and Healing Practices   40

Chapter 6. Special Needs and Issues of Veterans   **43**

   Female Veterans   49
   Gender Issues and Spirituality   51

Chapter 7. Pastoral Care Issues for the Pastor/Caregiver   **55**

   Role of the Pastor   55
   Gender Issues and Sexuality   59

Race, Class, and Cultural Issues   61
Alternative Spirituality   63
Suicide and Crisis Intervention   64

Chapter 8. Healing Rituals   **67**
A Liturgy of Communion and Healing   69

Chapter 9. Good News in Scripture   **77**

Chapter 10. Working with Therapists, Counselors,
and Doctors   **83**

Chapter 11. Clergy Self-Care   **89**

Chapter 12. Prevention of PTSD   **95**

Epilogue   **105**

Appendix. Spiritual Assessment   **107**

Bibliography   **109**

Index   **117**

Foreword

Having grown up with parents who had survived their own experiences of being psychologically and spiritually wounded one might expect that I would have been able to at least recognize such injuries. The truth was that, for the first thirty years of my life, I had no conscious awareness of what it meant to be wounded unless the wounds were visible. Nor were the seminary or other graduate programs that I later completed particularly helpful in teaching me to recognize, much less to help others to cope with, the symptoms of disorders such as post-traumatic stress disorder (PTSD). Not even following my ordination in 1981 was I taught about the complex psychological and spiritual consequences that often result from trauma sufficient to cause PTSD.

Reverend Daléne C. Fuller Rogers has written a concise but inclusive book about these psychological and spiritual consequences of trauma. Although initially focusing on sexual trauma, she clearly deals both with other sources of trauma as well as several dimensions of traumatic experiences. She incorporates the experiences of some of her earlier parishioners and hospital patients in ways that illustrate the complexity of this disorder.

Her treatment of the subject includes areas that need to be highlighted so that pastors are both enlightened and encouraged to respond as pastors to the spiritual needs of people who are traumatized. Reverend Fuller Rogers emphasizes the need for pastors to have thought through their own theologies about theodicy, suffering, and forgiveness. She urges pastors to consider both the limits to what they can offer their parishioners as well as the means to sustain themselves in dealing with the needs of those who were or are wounded by trauma. Particularly important is her emphasis on the need for pastors to have ongoing pastoral supervision so that they can process their own reactions to their parishioners' traumas—especially transference and projection.

In addition to her overall treatment of PTSD and to her exploration of several aspects of PTSD, Reverend Fuller Rogers clarifies the uncertainty that sometimes hinders pastors in their efforts to provide appropriate pastoral care. She encourages a partnership approach to help "heal the shattered soul" by walking with the wounded, empowering and supporting their recovery. In my experience, pastors are sometimes uncertain about their roles as pastoral caregivers and are all-too-easily convinced that they have little or nothing to offer a traumatized person. Hence, they are sometimes unwilling to accompany the wounded person along the journey that he or she makes with a counselor/therapist. Reverend Fuller Rogers urges pastors to "be there" for their parishioners. I strongly agree with her perspective.

Several places in the book demonstrate keen insight and make memorable statements. For example, in Chapter 4 she states, "A pastor should not be providing pastoral care alone." Although that may seem terribly obvious, I have known many pastors and congregations to whom that would be news. Then in Chapter 5 she asserts that "God will see to it that our wounds do not get the best of us." This is a remarkably candid theological assertion and one that is biblically grounded. In Chapter 6 she reminds the reader that "War devastates the soul." Every veteran I have ever met would agree with that statement, but many of the rest of us do not really understand the spiritual devastation wrought by war. Another valuable insight is in Chapter 7 when she writes: "All crises are spiritual at the core because they involve issues which call for reflection on one's values, purpose, and meaning in life." Truly, this is an insight that pastoral caregivers need to have at the very center of everything they do to help their parishioners/patients. Otherwise, the risk is great of overlooking the significance of the spiritual in their quest to understand the psychological and other dimensions of PTSD and its attendant spiritual wound.

The liturgy of communion and healing in Chapter 8 is a very well thought-out tool for offering traumatized persons a means to reconnect with a sacrament that was meant to bring the community of God's people together. The chapter on clergy self-care is also an important reminder that we who are clergy need to take care of ourselves or we simply will not have the inner resources with which to walk with those who suffer. I was particularly impressed with Reverend Fuller Rogers' understanding of "detachment": "But to me, detachment is a kind of letting go after a moment of compassion or empathy, when a pastor has experienced deep sharing and profound vulnerability. Detachment allows the pastor to leave the issue or the problem with the person after having embraced it together." We who provide pastoral care need this insight for we all-too-often hold on to our parishioner/patient's issue or problem and thus take another step along the road to burnout.

I recommend this book for anyone involved in the art of pastoral caregiving; especially pastors, religious educators, and youth group workers. I also recommend this book to seminary students, clinical pastoral education students, and chaplains. Finally, mental health professionals who wish to be sensitized to the spiritual dimensions of PTSD and the pastoral care of those who suffer from it would profit from reading this book as well.

Chaplain Lawrence L. LaPierre, DMin, BCC
Retired Chief, Chaplain Service
VA Medical and Regional Office Center
White River Junction, Vermont

Acknowledgments

It is impossible to express adequately my gratitude to the survivors of trauma who have allowed me to be their pastor. I have learned more about the spirituality of healing from survivors themselves than from all the textbooks I have read.

I am also greatly indebted to the faculty and students of the Episcopal Divinity School, Cambridge, Massachusetts, for opening my eyes to the prevalence of abuse, and for providing me with the training necessary to direct my passion for peace and justice. Specifically, I am grateful to the patience and wisdom of the Reverend Dr. Suzanne Hiatt, the Reverend Dr. Carter Heyward, the Reverend Dr. Alison Cheek, the Reverend Dr. Katie Geneva Cannon, Dr. Joanna Dewey, and the late Reverend Dr. Donald Winslow. Student colleagues who stand out in my memory for challenging my assumptions and ignorance are Laura Ruth Garrett, Bev Bryant, and David Gellatly.

I am also grateful to the companions I have had along the way who have supported me through seminary, been a pastor to the pastor, and listened to my crises of faith: my daughters, Carolyn and Kristen; special friends: the late Rina Glover, Reverend Marjorie MacNeill, Reverend Nancy Shepherd, Sue Gleason, Reverend Betty Long, and Reverend William Heuss, and the congregation of the Church of the Good Shepherd, Acton, Massachusetts.

My ministry as a chaplain to veterans has been supported, informed, and supervised by the Reverend Dr. Lawrence LaPierre, whose experience, insight, and wisdom have been invaluable to his staff.

Finally, the support and encouragement I needed to bring this book from an idea to a reality came from my partner Susan Pelley. Her editing and thoughtful critique has contributed to the clarity of the text.

Chapter 1

Defining Post-Traumatic Stress Disorder and Its Causes

Evil is a temporary rebellion against the love of God.

Morton T. Kelsey

Identification of the effects of trauma on the human psyche has a long history, It was not until 1980, however, that the term "post-traumatic stress disorder" (PTSD) first appeared in the third edition of the *Diagnostic and Statistical Manual of Mental Disorders* (DSM-III). As early as the nineteenth century, PTSD was described as the "effort syndrome," "DaCosta's syndrome," and "railway spine." After World War I, symptoms in soldiers returning from active duty were identified as "shell shock," and "soldier's heart." Since then, it has been common to find such terms as "combat fatigue," "combat neurosis," "postrape syndrome," "post-Vietnam syndrome," "accident neurosis," and "compensation neurosis." Though references to PTSD are more common today, recognition, understanding, and treatment of the disease has progressed slowly.

PTSD has very specific characteristics. The DSM-IV-TR (2000) describes a complex assessment of symptoms beginning with the precipitating event:

> . . . exposure to an extreme traumatic stressor involving direct personal experience of an event that involves actual or threatened death or serious injury, or other threat to one's physical integrity; or witnessing an event that involves death, injury, or a threat to the physical integrity of another person; or learning about unexpected or violent death, serious harm, or threat of death or injury experience by a family member or other close as-

sociate (Criterion A1) (p. 463). Reprinted with permission from the *Diagnostic and Statistical Manual of Mental Disorders, Fourth Edition, Text Revision.* Copyright 2000 American Psychiatric Association.

The traumatic event is something extraordinary, not within the range of typical human experience. The threat or actual harm may be directed at one's partner, children, close friends, or relatives. The threat or harm may carry such consequences as destruction of one's property or neighborhood. Seeing another person become a victim of a traumatic event can result in PTSD in the witness, as well as in the victim.

PTSD affects hundreds of thousands of people around the world who have been victims of, or witnesses to, such horrors as "rape, domestic violence, child abuse, war, accidents, natural disasters and political torture" (American Psychological Association Public Information, PTSD, Accessed: www.APA.org, p. 1). Both males and females are affected at all age levels.

The traumatic events that can produce PTSD can be divided into three categories:

1. *Natural disasters:* hurricanes, tornadoes, floods, earthquakes, forest fires, volcanic eruptions
2. *Accidental human-made disasters:* auto crashes, nuclear power plant accidents, industrial accidents, airplane crashes, house fires, train derailments
3. *Intentional human-made disasters:* war/military combat, terrorist bombings, rape, ritual abuse, muggings, assault, armed robbery, stalking, hazing, multiple forms of verbal, physical, sexual, and emotional abuse such as domestic battering and violence in schools

Perhaps the essential description of traumatic or "terrorizing" conditions that lead to PTSD comes from Judith Lewis Herman in her book *Trauma and Recovery* (1992): "Psychological trauma is an affliction of the powerless. At the moment of trauma, the victim is rendered helpless by overwhelming force. . . . Traumatic events overwhelm the ordinary systems of care that give people a sense of control, connection, and meaning" (p. 32).

SEXUAL TRAUMA

Rape

Survivors of rape, the crime of forcing another person to submit to sex acts, have a high occurrence of PTSD. Rape is a multidimensional trauma violating the spiritual, physical, and psychological boundaries of a person. According to the National Crime Victimization Survey, Bureau of Justice Statistics, U.S. Department of Justice (1997), between 1995 and 1996, more than 670,000 women were victims of rape, attempted rape, or sexual assault. In 1995, 32,130 males age twelve and older were victims of rape, attempted rape, or sexual assault.

Marital Rape

Sexual activity must be consensual to be a truly mutual, pleasurable experience. When any sexual activity is forced upon one's spouse by threat, intimidation, physical overpowering, or any unwanted means, it may be considered rape, even within the context of a legal marriage.

The incidence of marital rape is believed to be grossly underreported because many women have been psychologically conditioned to assume that their husbands have a right to demand sexual participation and to expect them to engage in sexual activity regardless of whether they want to participate.

Until the late 1970s, most states did not consider spousal rape a crime. By mid-1982, eleven states had laws that treated rape by a husband or cohabitator the same as rape by a stranger. Some thirty also permitted marital rape charges under some circumstances (Boston Women's Health Book Collective, 1984). Ongoing political action on behalf of women's rights on July 5, 1993, created legislation making marital rape a crime in all fifty states, under at least one section of the sexual offense codes. There are no exceptions from rape prosecution granted to husbands in seventeen states and the District of Columbia. However, in thirty-three states, there are still some exemptions from rape prosection given to husbands. When his wife is unable to consent, in such conditions as mental or physical impairment, or asleep or unconscious, a husband is exempt from prosecution in many of these thirty-three states. While spousal rape is now considered a crime, victims often have to overcome legal hurdles to prosecution not present for other victims of rape (Bergen, 1999, p. 2).

Incest

Sexual activity between family members is the traditional definition of incest. However, each state legally defines incest differently. When considering the social attitudes of our culture about incest, it is most frequently defined as the occurrence of sexual activity between older male relatives and younger females in families of every class and color.

> Because it happens within the family context, an incestuous relationship is one over which a child or young woman has no control. A trusted family member uses his power—as well as love and dependence to initiate sexual contact, and to insure also that the relationship continues and remains secret. (Boston Women's Health Collective, 1984, p. 109)

Many young boys and girls do not tell anyone about the incest until their adult years when memories may become vivid and interfere with a healthy sex life with their partner of choice. Many teenagers who have been victims of incest run away, become sexually promiscuous to feel accepted, or become depressed and turn to drugs and alcohol. Most victims have a damaged sense of self-worth and self-esteem.

Cult/Ritual Abuse

Ritual abuse is sadistic and humiliating trauma that is systematic and recurrent, and utilizes techniques such as conditioning, torture, and mind control to damage the physical, sexual, spiritual, and/or emotional health of a person. It is unusual for this form of abuse to be a single incident. The victims are children, adolescents, and adults regardless of gender.

Genital Mutilation

The practice of female circumcision is a traditional cultural ritual in many African countries, where as many as 20 million to 74 million females, mostly young girls, undergo some form of genital surgery every year. Unknown numbers of girls are circumcised in Indonesia and Malaysia. As people from these cultures immigrate to the United States, doctors are beginning to discover evidence of genital mutilations being performed here.

> The mildest form of reduction is circumcision, which involves cutting off the hood of the clitoris. This is often called sunna, or traditional circumcision. The next level of removal is excision, or clitoridectomy, which involves cutting off part or all of the clitoris and part or all of the labia minora. Even more extreme is infibulation, in which part of all of the middle section of the labia majora is also cut off. The two sides of the vulva are then pinned together with catgut or silk sutures, leaving a small opening for menstrual blood and urine. While not as common, infibulation is still widely practiced in Africa. (Boston Women's Health Collective, 1984, p. 617)

The medical and health consequences to these practices can be devastating. It is more difficult to assess the psychosocial and spiritual consequences to the women and girls because circumcision is deeply ingrained in the culture in the countries where it originates. In native circumstances, it is often considered a basic part of a young girl's rite of passage and is viewed as evidence of their womanhood. As more women begin to be educated about the life-threatening aspects of this practice and the damaging effects to a woman's organs, their resistance to female circumcision is rising. Some women and their young daughters have sought asylum in other countries to escape the demands of their community to have this procedure performed. Although we in the white-dominated Western culture must resist imposing our cultural values on others, it is essential that we have an awareness of the existence of such practices, and their impact on women spiritually as we become a more multicultural, multiracial society, and church.

PHYSICAL TRAUMA

Men are more likely than women to experience combat trauma, torture (prisoners of war), and physical attacks than women. However, women are reported to be victims of rape, sexual molestation, and physical abuse as children in greater numbers than men (Solomon and Davidson, 1997). "The most common traumatic events (affecting about 15 percent to 35 percent of the people surveyed) were witnessing someone badly injured or killed; being involved in a fire, flood, or natural disaster; and being involved in a life-threatening accident" (1997, p. 6). Physical trauma is usually a dominant aspect of domestic violence, ritual abuse, and elder abuse. School violence usually involves physical fights or shoving and pushing. Occasionally, a knife or other weapon may be used. Gang violence frequently involves weapons, intimidation, and fear.

People who have been subjected to physical trauma of any kind may develop PTSD, especially if the physical trauma took place over a long time. One of the lingering effects of physical and sexual trauma is a distrust of physical contact. Body boundaries have been violated, and it takes time for victims to fully regain a level of comfort with even nonsexual touching. Therefore, it is important for pastors to know that expressions of physical contact such as the "passing of the peace" during a worship service can be difficult for some survivors. Well-meaning, friendly parishioners may routinely greet people with a hug without asking first if this is acceptable. Pastors should model sensitivity in this area and teach their congregations to be aware of the need for physical boundaries.

On the other hand, from a spiritual perspective, safe touch is vital to emotional and physical health and well-being. Our American culture has a reputation for low rates of loving, nonsexual touch between friends and family members. Learning to receive touch from a nonthreatening person is part of a trauma victim's healing process. Pastors have a responsibility to be boundary sensitive and should be alert to body language and other nonverbal gestures that signal refusal to accept handshaking or an embrace. Standing too close to a person may also make them uncomfortable. Sometimes a trusted pastor may be chosen by a survivor as a safe individual to begin to reestablish comfort with nonsexual touch. This is a potentially risky area for pastors because of their own boundary issues. If a pastor has weak boundaries, combined with a high degree of power, a greater possibility exists of clergy misconduct occurring. A comprehensive analysis of this issue may be found by reading *Is Nothing Sacred?* (1989), by Reverend Marie Fortune.

PSYCHOLOGICAL TRAUMA

The most common psychological trauma in cases of natural disaster, combat, hostage taking, prisoners of war, rape, ritual abuse, domestic violence, child abuse, elder abuse, and school or gang violence where life is threatened is PTSD. Occasionally, in cases of hostages, POWs, kidnapping, child abuse, elder abuse, and domestic violence, we see what is called the "Stockholm syndrome."

The term Stockholm syndrome came about in the aftermath of a 1973 hostage-taking episode in one of Stockholm's largest banks. Three women and one man were taken hostage. During the six days they were held by two ex-convicts, their lives were threatened, but they were also shown kindness. Surprisingly, all of the hostages defended their captors and strongly resisted their government's efforts to rescue them. The hostages were rescued by police and several months later were reported to continue to have warm feelings toward the men who had threatened their lives, raised money for their captors' defense, and two of the women became engaged to marry the two captors.

After the Stockholm incident, social scientists began to investigate whether the bonding between the hostages and their captors was an isolated experience or a common feeling in oppressive situations. It has been determined that the Stockholm syndrome is a survival mechanism that comes into play when people are fighting for their lives. It has happened to prisoners of war, battered women, kidnapped children, incest victims, physically and/or emotionally abused children, cult members, concentration camp prisoners, etc. Adaptation to the abusive environment is the means of survival. Anyone may manifest the Stockholm syndrome if the following conditions are met:

- Captives perceive their survival is threatened, and they believe that the captor is capable of acting on the threat.
- Captives are terrorized and perceive receiving small kindnesses from the captor.
- Captives are isolated from hearing perceptions other than the captor's.
- Captives perceive no possibility of escape.

It usually takes three or four days of these conditions for the psychological shift to be completed. Following release from captivity, depression and PTSD are likely to be manifested in the victims.

Pastors can expect some members of their congregations who have been subjected to child abuse and domestic violence to have coped through the psychological survival mechanism of the Stockholm syndrome. For pastors, understanding the syndrome may help them be more compassionate when observing how difficult it may be for a woman to leave her batterer and why she often returns to the life-threatening relationship, for example. When victims become aware of the Stockholm syndrome it helps their spiritual healing as they begin to see that the battering was not their fault.

SPIRITUAL TRAUMA

All forms of trauma—sexual, physical, and psychological—have an effect on one's spirituality. Some people have said that spiritual trauma has had the most lasting and devastating impact on their lives. I believe the symptoms and manifestations of PTSD (see Chapters 2 and 3) reflect the spirit's wounding and cry for healing.

Spiritual trauma attacks the core of one's being; one's relationship to God and the relationship to oneself. The meaning and purpose of life becomes vague, confused, or lost. The ability to connect with nature, mystery, love, people, the transcendent, is ruptured, and the effects of such brokenness surface.

Some of the ways that spiritual trauma attacks a person's well-being are as follows:

- Loss of self-worth; feelings of being unlovable
- Shame
- Confusion
- Powerlessness; helplessness
- Self-doubt; self-critical and judgmental
- Depression
- Sense of being out of balance
- Negativity; nothing feels right
- Difficulty with boundaries; setting them/respecting them
- Self-directed anger
- Lack of meaning and purpose in life; feeling empty

- Loss of intimacy; breakdown in relationships: with others and with the divine/sacred
- Suffering without meaning
- Diminished ability to feel pleasure or love

When the source of trauma has been clergy sexual abuse, ritual abuse, or participation in religious cults, a person's alienation from God and anger directed toward God can be profound. Usually this is accompanied by a crisis in faith, if not a loss of faith and anger directed at organized religion and its representatives, i.e., clergy and lay leaders. Sometimes it is helpful for the victims of this type of trauma to hear religious leaders and clergy acknowledge that abuse does occur in religious settings and communities, and that the church should be held accountable.

Some victims feel the need to stay away from organized religion entirely. Others return to express their anger to the institution. This can be disruptive to the faith community, but it also provides an opportunity for healing.

One of the ways a pastor may respond to these situations that has been found to be effective is to invite the survivor of clergy sexual abuse, ritual abuse, or cult trauma to help the church create abuse-prevention guidelines if they are not already established. Discussion of organizing a healing circle that culminates in a healing ceremony may also be useful (see Chapter 8). Exploring and discussing the meaning and purpose of forgiveness can be extremely helpful, if the timing is right, but no one should be pushed into forgiveness.

Sometimes a person is not ready to attend worship services, but may benefit from reading literature that addresses spiritual and faith issues. Several excellent resources are listed in the bibliography of this book. Attending workshops on spiritual abuse with a survivor can be mutually beneficial for pastors and survivors. It is also an important act of support when a pastor leads his or her church by recommending that funds be set aside for victims to attend healing seminars. The ideal, however, is to eliminate the source of trauma. Pastors should be vocal and active in their local communities in combating the causes of trauma and violence. Chapter 12 addresses ways to do this.

EYEWITNESSES AND SURVIVORS OF DISASTER

Symptoms of PTSD may be seen in people who have witnessed the suffering or death of other people. Survivors of a natural disaster, war/combat, or other forms of mass annihilation are likely to experience "survivor guilt"—the burden of the knowledge that they were spared when others around them were dying. "They feel guilty for not risking their lives to save others, or for failing to fulfill the request of a dying person" (Herman, 1992, p. 54).

Witnessing the death of a loved one in a natural disaster, or a soldier who witnesses the death of a buddy in combat, are events that have a strong likelihood of leading to a trauma syndrome. Children who witness violence between their parents, even if they are not physically abused themselves, suffer from the exposure, which threatens their own sense of safety and trust. Rescue teams of "first responders" to natural disasters, even medical professionals, may experience short-term posttrauma effects as a result of viewing severely injured or dismembered bodies. The impact may be related to the number of victims or to the intensity and length of time over which the harm occurred. Eyewitnesses to shootings, homicides, beatings, gang violence, ritual abuse, etc., will be adversely affected to some degree depending on their relationship with the victims.

In an interview with Rabbi Earl A. Grollman, best-selling author on grief counseling, published in *World,* the journal of the Unitarian Universalist Association (July/August, 2000), Dan Kennedy reported Grollman's reaction to his counseling work at the site of the Oklahoma federal building bombing in 1995:

> It was horrifying. The enormity of it overpowered me. You're not dealing with one or two or five—it's 169 people . . . the bombing took its toll on me. The hardest thing was that when I returned to Boston, I couldn't rid myself of the smell of burning bodies. How do clergy and grief counselors handle our pain? Most of us who are great with everybody else don't know what to do with ourselves. (p. 19)

Pastors may be called upon to offer pastoral support and care to those who have witnessed a violent event. They may have to remain calm and composed while listening to horrific accounts of death and suffering. Pastors and chaplains should be prepared to cope with their own responses of helplessness, disgust, fear, and anger toward the survivor or the person(s) who hurt them. Posttrauma reflection may bring up deep questions about the meaning of suffering, God's power, and love. Some of the theological dimensions of trauma, and how a pastor who has dealt with these issues can support spiritual healing are addressed in Chapter 5.

Chapter 2

Symptoms of PTSD

To enter into the presence of another human being is to enter into the presence of God in a new and different way. . . . We must come into the presence of our fellow human beings with a sense of awe and gratitude.

Stephen Carter

According to the DSM-IV-TR diagnostic criteria, a person who has exhibited the symptoms of PTSD for a month or longer qualifies for a PTSD diagnosis. If the symptoms are present for four weeks or less and appear resolved within that time frame, a diagnosis of acute stress disorder will be made. The PTSD is considered chronic if unresolved in three months or more. The DSM-IV-TR also acknowledges that the symptom of PTSD may appear long after the actual trauma occurs. The term "delayed onset" is used to describe symptoms arising at least six months after the traumatic event.

Identification and diagnosis of PTSD is dependent upon a continued reexperiencing of the traumatic incident. The diagnostic criteria from the DSM-IV-TR (309.81) (APA, 2000) require reexperiencing in one or more of these ways:

1. Recurrent and intrusive distressing recollections of the event, including images, thoughts, or perceptions (*Note:* In young children, repetitive play may occur in which themes or aspects of the trauma are expressed.)
2. Recurrent distressing dreams of the event (*Note:* In children, there may be frightening dreams without recognizable content.)
3. Acting or feeling as if the traumatic event were recurring (includes a sense of reliving the experience, illusions, hallucinations, and dissociative flashback episodes, including those that

occur on awakening or when intoxicated) (*Note:* In young children, trauma-specific reenactment may occur.)
4. Intense psychological distress at exposure to internal or external cues that symbolize or resemble an aspect of the traumatic event
5. Physiological reactivity on exposure to internal or external cues that symbolize or resemble an aspect of the traumatic event

Another required behavioral symptom for diagnosis is persistent avoidance of thoughts and activities related to the trauma and signs of the numbing of one's reactions (not present before the trauma). The specific criteria require that three or more of the following be present:

1. Efforts to avoid thoughts, feeling, or conversations associated with the trauma
2. Efforts to avoid activities, places, or people that arouse recollections of the trauma
3. Inability to recall an important aspect of the trauma
4. Markedly diminished interest or participation in significant activities
5. Feeling of detachment or estrangement from others
6. Restricted range of affect (e.g., unable to have loving feelings)
7. Sense of a foreshortened future (e.g., does not expect to have a career, marriage, children, or a normal life span)

Other behaviors indicative of increased arousal are also required for a definitive diagnosis. Two or more of the following indicators must be present:

1. Difficulty falling or staying asleep
2. Irritability or outbursts of anger
3. Difficulty concentrating
4. Hypervigilance
5. Exaggerated startle response. Reprinted with permission from the *Diagnostic and Statistical Manual of Mental Disorders, Fourth Edition, Text Revision.* Copyright 2000 American Psychiatric Association.

These clear, well-defined criteria are followed by most mental health treatment centers for purposes of medical insurance reimbursement. They are also an attempt to produce an accurate diagnosis and understanding of certain behavioral characteristics exhibited after a traumatic event. However, they have their limitations. It is possible to have an experience that is traumatizing, but which is being expressed with symptoms in different combinations than the DSM-IV-TR criteria allows. Traumatic events can be ruining your life, yet you may not qualify for a PTSD diagnosis. The range of reactions to trauma is broad and related to a person's history, skills, and differing emotional and spiritual capacities.

What is important for the pastor is the ability to respond with understanding and compassion to any woman, man, or child who has experienced trauma from a human act, violence, or a natural disaster. Knowing the kinds of treatment, services, and supports that contribute to recovery can make a significant difference in a survivor's life. Without timely intervention, experiences of violence can crush a person's spirit and lead to use of drugs and alcohol. Substance abuse often includes encounters with the criminal justice system.

Recovery will take patience and persistence on the part of the survivor and the pastor or chaplain. The psychological issues of trauma survivors may make it difficult for them to hear and process the information they need to heal. Sometimes this is misinterpreted as resistance. To begin healing, survivors will need people who can listen to their recollections and help them vocalize their feelings, which may be difficult and deeply painful to express.

Members of the victim's family can also play an important role in encouraging the individual to seek help, and by providing support during the recovery and treatment process. The pastor and the faith community can be essential contributors to making the time of healing an opportunity for growth and deeper bonding for all involved.

Chapter 3

Common Manifestations

The man who opts for revenge should dig two graves.

Chinese Proverb

It is normal to be affected by trauma and violence. The manifestations of PTSD lead to complications in socializing and may interfere with relationships, but at the time they first arise their purpose is survival. What later may be judged as weird and inappropriate behavior was an effective biological-based response to life-threatening stressors at the time of the traumatic event.

A survivor may experience interrupted sleep because at the time of the trauma it was not safe to be asleep. Sleep disturbance, especially when it involves nightmares, can create stress in marital and other partnered relationships. Both persons may end up suffering from sleep deprivation. Some Vietnam veterans continue to have occasional dreams that cause them to shake during the middle of the night. It is not unusual for a combat veteran to awaken suddenly from sleep and find his hands around the neck of the person in bed with him. Those who refuse to seek professional help often turn to alcohol abuse in a futile attempt to cope.

For some, hypervigilance is another means of survival; being alert and ready, searching for something dangerous to happen at any time. When someone is hypervigilant and anxious, it will be difficult, if not impossible, to relax and enjoy a movie in a theater or a family gathering. Being in unfamiliar surroundings will increase anxiety. Lack of sleep and hypervigilance makes it hard to concentrate on everyday things. The ability to concentrate on reading or studying may be poor. If the survivor is a student, he or she may be labeled unintelligent or as having a learning disorder, when the real problem is PTSD.

Survivors may also startle easily. I attended seminary with a Chilean woman who grew up during the oppression and civil wars of the Pinochet regime. She would jump and a look of fear would cross her face, as though she was ready to seek cover, whenever a car would backfire or a fire alarm or rescue vehicle siren would sound. I also learned quickly as a veterans administration (VA) hospital chaplain to avoid accidentally bumping the bed of a sleeping patient, and never to touch the veterans until after awakening them by calling out their names. Well-meaning nurses without such awareness have been known to be grabbed and choked as a result of activation of the vet's startle response.

Irritability or difficulty regulating anger is a common manifestation of PTSD. Some people seem to vacillate between outbursts of rage and periods of numbing behavior. Events in the present that are reminders of the past trauma can trigger anxiety, anger, rage, flashbacks, and other PTSD symptoms. Common triggers are anniversary dates of the traumatic event, people, and places, and objects that carry some similar feature to the original trauma.

Generally speaking, our culture is more accepting of males expressing anger than females. Therefore, when supporting females with anger control issues, cultural and religious attitudes must be taken into consideration. When men are angry and enraged, it is not helpful to their recovery to ignore it as just part of what men are like. Anger, as well as grief are symptoms of much more complex issues.

SPIRITUAL ISSUES: GRIEF AND ANGER

The process of mourning traumatic losses takes longer, for example, than the expected death of an ill, elderly loved one. Although everyone's grieving and mourning times are different, a survivor will need more than two years to mourn traumatic losses. Progressing in therapy will be difficult until grieving begins.

Grief is exhausting and may create extreme emotional and spiritual suffering. There may be a desire to drop out of counseling because it is "too hard," but the only way out is to move through the stages of grief. Unexpressed sorrow and incomplete grief can lead to the development or exacerbation of medical problems such as hypertension, heart disease, asthma, diabetes, fibromyalgia, arthritis, and irritable bowel syndrome. To avoid grief is to risk repressing anger and sorrow and remaining stuck with the behavioral patterns of unresolved grief. Survivors may be more willing to yield to the pain and suffering that surface during the grief process if they know they will have a comforter, a companion on that journey. The pastor may serve directly, walking with the wounded person, or the pastor may be the one who offers pastoral care to the survivors' partner, spouse, or best friend. Therefore, it is wise for pastors to be familiar with the levels of loss and the stages of grief, especially as they apply to survivors.

Levels of Loss

Tangible Losses

Three major levels of loss have been identified by Aphrodite Matsakis (1994): "The first level is the loss of specific people or things or the physical, emotional, or spiritual aspects of the self that have been lost" (p. 260). The tangible kind of losses may be obvious, such as the loss of a body part, or the loss of one's house, or the death of a loved one. A change in one's mental or physical ability, such as the inability to express or enjoy sexual intimacy, can be experienced as the death of a part of the self. Less apparent losses can be comparable in their impact.

Trauma survivors may lose faith in God and lack a sense of awe and wonder about creation. They may disavow the goodness of humanity and the integrity of the agencies or people connected to the traumatic event. Spiritual losses also may be reflected in a lack of hope in the future, the loss of trust, a sense of no longer being a whole person, the inability to respond spontaneously and optimistically, and the loss of childlike innocence. Thus, the role of the pastor is to help survivors identify the spirituality that gave their lives meaning before being traumatized and to guide them in recreating a spirituality from their new, revised perspectives and understandings as wounded persons. The spiritual losses may be less visible but to the survivor they may be the most devastating.

Loss of Control

The second level of loss concerns loss of control. Some losses cannot be replaced or restored regardless of what attempts are made.

Some of the wounds of trauma leave scars that may never fully heal, so survivors will need to confront their powerlessness and begin to learn how to live with their lasting reminders of loss.

"Survivors of family traumas such as child abuse, battering, suicide, and so on, need to mourn the loss of the dream of the ideal family they always desired" (Matsakis, 1994, p. 261). They will need to come to grips with the reality that they are powerless to create change in their family members. This loss will need to be grieved for the survivor to be freed to meet their own needs.

Confronting Mortality

Confronting mortality is the third level of loss. In our culture, we avoid, at all costs, thinking and speaking about death; the final letting go can be viewed spiritually as complete freedom but also as the utter loss of all control—complete powerlessness. As the survivor faces the death of others and parts of oneself, mortality must be seen as a certainty. The pastor can offer assistance in exploring the spiritual issues and questions surrounding death, such as pain, suffering, resurrection, afterlife, heaven, hell, and judgment.

The Grieving Process

The grieving process has been delineated to involve five stages according to Elizabeth Kübler-Ross in her classic book *On Death and Dying* (1969): denial, anger, bargaining, depression, and acceptance. These stages may be experienced in any order, for any length of time, and the stages may overlap one another. People who are suffering a significant loss, as well as people who are dying, can be expected to show signs of the five stages of grief.

Denial

Denial is similar to shock. It is a psychological defense in which one refuses to acknowledge that the trauma or loss occurred or that it had any adverse effect. Someone who has witnessed others suffer trauma may feel like it was "all a bad dream." It is possible to be stuck in denial for many years.

Anger

After denial is dealt with, anger may flood to the surface. This is when the survivor may express anger at God or at life. If the trauma was inflicted by an individual, the survivor may become enraged at the perpetrator and seek revenge. Sometimes the anger may be turned toward the self as the survivor feels responsible for allowing or accepting the trauma. It may take time for patient processing before the survivors can see that they were powerless, at the time, to do anything but accept it.

Bargaining

Bargaining is the stage of grief that reflects on the "if only" and "what if" of trauma situations. This process may be useful if a person was responsible for traumatizing another person. However, for victims to inflict self-blame through the what-ifs and if-onlys, they will create barriers to their healing process. Getting a realistic perspective on what truly happened will be more helpful.

Depression

Depression takes many forms. There are the normal variations in mood that most people experience as part of daily life. Clinical depression, on the other hand, interferes with a person's ability to function and cope. Symptoms of clinical depression may include: loss of concentration, changes in sleeping and eating habits, increase in physical illnesses, despair and loss of hope in the future, loss of interest in physical appearance, decreased libido, excessive fatigue, or restlessness.

Depression is a normal response to loss and is part of the grieving process. Although the depression that comes with grief is temporary, it may be intense and psychologically and spiritually painful. It is common for grief-related depression to be associated with many of the symptoms of clinical depression previously outlined. If the pastor recognizes the symptoms of clinical depression in a grieving person, it would be wise to recommend the person to a mental health counselor for a professional evaluation.

Acceptance

The final stage of grief is acceptance. Once individuals have processed their way through the other stages, not necessarily in the order presented, they will reach a place where they acknowledge and accept the consequences and effects of the loss on their life and those whose lives intersect with them. At this point, they accept their grief and that the loss can never be replaced, but that they can learn to live with it.

Each time a person experiences a new loss, previous losses may be recalled and regrieved. Every time this happens, the pain is relieved a little more. Reassurances that what may feel like an overreaction to a loss is simply the compounding of experiences that may help the grieving person understand his or her intense feelings.

The culture in which a person lives imposes expectations about the grieving process. Cultural restrictions about expressing emotions may create barriers to the grief process. Stoicism is usually considered the proper response to loss in our Western, white society. Some people may resist expressing their emotions out of fear of being judged as lacking self-control. Employers may consider the grieving person to be a liability or incompetent to perform his or her job. When my husband died suddenly, leaving me alone to support and to raise my two daughters, ages five and seven, I had been home from my job for two consecutive weeks before I could begin to imagine having enough physical energy, emotional stability, and mental acuity to return to my work as a nuclear medicine technologist. During that time, my supervisor called me every two days asking how much more time I would have to be away from my responsibilities. He never acknowledged the suddenness or significance of my loss, nor did he ask about my network of support. I felt pressured to pull myself together and get back on the job or risk being fired. This personal experience is a reminder of the broad range that a loss encompasses. Identifying the extent of one's loss requires examining the spiritual, emotional, financial, physical, social, and moral implications.

The pastor who can accept, support, and affirm a person through all the stages and complications of grief is offering critical pastoral care. Providing a safe environment in which to cry, scream, and vent the intense emotions that grief may present is a great gift. I remember visiting with a young widow in her home several times during the first month after her husband's sudden death in a motor vehicle accident. She and I did not spend much time in conversation during those visits. It seemed that I was fulfilling a need by stopping in, offering a soft hug, drinking tea, and sitting beside her on the sofa. We began and ended my visit with prayer. During one of those visits, I recall her saying that she felt as though she "saved up" her tears for when I was there because I was the only one who did not tell her to stop crying or try to get on with her life for the sake of the children. This reinforced for me the value of pastoral care and support that is offered by simply being present and avoiding the desire to fix someone's situation or make them feel better. Sacred time, healing time, may be most powerful when few words are spoken, but hearts and spirits are joined.

Anger

For those who have a history of trauma, anger is intense. Angry people are not easy to be around, and even those who care greatly about the survivor, with knowledge about PTSD, may find they are tested to their limits by the survivor's rage and unpredictability. Whether survivors express their anger or turn it inward at themselves, they can benefit from anger management techniques taught by a counselor.

The pastoral caregiver may want to approach the survivor about reflecting on the spiritual nature of the anger. Does the anger feel empowering or is it taking energy away? Is the survivor able to use the anger constructively, or is the anger in control of the survivor? Sometimes anger is just a symptom of some other underlying feeling. The survivor may benefit from exploring what other feelings are present with the anger such as sadness, fatigue, job-related stress. *When Anger Hurts* (McKay, Rogers, and McKay, 1989), is an excellent source on anger and its management.

The pastor may discover that some survivors have been raised to believe that all anger is sinful and wrong. This may lead survivors to suppress their anger, putting them at higher risk for clinical depression. If the survivor is motivated by religious teachings, it is helpful for the pastor to offer examples of appropriate expression of anger sanctioned by God in scripture (see Chapter 9). It may be helpful for pastors to acknowledge that they get angry and explain ways they have found useful to express it. Once a person can see the spiritual component to anger, and the meaning it may reveal, the easier it may become to deal with it. Receiving affirmation that God understands their anger, and that God can also deal with being the target of anger, may bring survivors some relief.

While offering insight and support around the issue of anger, the pastor should not cross the line into attempting anything therapeutic with survivors, and if survivors refuse to discuss anger because they fear they may lose control and hurt someone or themselves, the pastor must not try to push for more information. Stick to the areas that are comfortable for the survivors to deal with, and which fall into the area of spiritual growth.

Chapter 4

Psychological Complications

In a world of broken trust, community is sustained by forgiveness.

Unknown

Psychological pain is intense following a traumatic event. One epidemiologic survey indicated that up to 80 percent of individuals with PTSD also meet the criteria for at least one other psychiatric diagnosis (Kessler, Sonnega, Bromet et al., 1995). A pastor is likely to be witness to a survivor's attempts to cope with the symptoms and manifestations of PTSD through the abuse of drugs or alcohol to numb the psychological pain. Sometimes the use of pills and alcohol are combined. Panic disorders and obsessive-compulsive behaviors are also common. According to therapist E. Sue Blume (1990), dissociation is more common in victims of childhood abuse than in victims of other types of trauma. Many incest survivors describe this behavior as "splitting," likening it to an out-of-body experience. Sometimes an adult who is recalling a childhood trauma in the form of a flashback, or who is experiencing stress in the present, will dissociate. For a survivor of incest, dissociation may occur during sexual activity with a safe partner. This can be a terrifying experience.

At one time in my ministry, I was providing pastoral support to a parishioner who had begun to deal with flashbacks from early childhood sexual abuse by her grandfather. She was married and the mother of two young daughters who were about the age that she was when she first experienced incest. Gina (not her real name) and her family were active members of the church. Her faith was a source of comfort to her as she went through the process of recalling the trauma, and Gina often spent time praying in the sanctuary, where she felt safe.

The church was open during my office hours, and anyone could come into the sanctuary without my seeing them from inside my office. My attention was suddenly drawn to sounds I heard coming from the sanctuary. I entered the room and found Gina curled up in a fetal position in a pew. She was shaking, crying, rocking, and mumbling over and over, "Please don't hurt Gina. Please don't hurt Gina." It quickly became clear to me that Gina was having a flashback.

Because of my training in dealing with survivors of sexual trauma, I knew of a few ways to help Gina regain control of her situation. I slowly approached Gina in the pew but did not touch her. I spoke to her, letting her know who I was. I told her she was with me in the church sanctuary, that she was having a flashback, and that she was safe now. I noticed that her eyes were tightly shut, and since it helps to use the five senses to regain orientation to the present, I asked her to look at me. This did not come easily for Gina; she seemed to have trouble hearing me, she was so deeply entrenched in the flashback. She was shaking and her breathing was not normal.

Next, I invited her to breathe deeply with me, encouraging her over and over to take deep breaths and to look at me, reassuring her that she was safe. Eventually she began to take a few deep breaths and she opened her eyes and saw me. I offered to let her hold my hand, which she grabbed tightly, and I asked her to put her feet on the floor so she could feel that she was sitting in a church pew. I asked her to look at the room so she could see she was in the sanctuary. I told her that her "little girl" was not alone, and that I would stay with her while she was letting go of her memories of the past. As we continued to breathe deeply together, I reminded her to keep her eyes open and to take in her location. The intensity of the flashback began to subside, and Gina gradually returned to the present.

It takes some time to transition from such a powerful experience. Gina needed to sit for a while before she felt able to move to my office where I offered her a soft chair and a blanket to wrap around herself, as she was feeling cold. She accepted my offer of a cup of tea. I gave her reassurance that what she had just experienced was a sign of her healing process in action. Gina was exhausted and needed some quiet time to restore herself before she was able to drive home.

When someone is experiencing a flashback, it is as if he or she is experiencing the trauma for the first time. For the pastor who has never witnessed someone in the midst of a flashback, it can be frightening and overwhelming. The pastor should realize that this is not a psychotic reaction; it shows the person is strong enough to confront traumatic memories. Helping a person in the middle of a flashback to get grounded again requires calmness, clarity, gentleness, and firmness from the pastor or friend. Sensitivity to the process and understanding of what is going on will convey reassurance to the survivor. The pastor who can recognize the reexperiencing process as a normal part of recovery and healing will make a great contribution to the person's sense of hope and self-acceptance.

Bulimic bingeing and anorexic starvation are also seen in sexual abuse survivors. Both are attempts to numb feelings and give the illusion of control over anxieties and emotions. The need to ease the painful feelings associated with the trauma makes a survivor vulnerable to other addictions such as drugs and alcohol. Addictive diseases affect a person physically, emotionally, mentally, and spiritually. Addiction to drugs and/or alcohol must be treated first before the survivor will make any headway in addressing deeper issues. It is useless for a pastor or other caregiver to urge an addict to stop after one or two drinks. The pastor will be powerless over the addict's behavior. The most caring thing a pastor can do, which will avoid a codependent relationship, is to show concern for the struggle but to be honest with the survivor about how one's behavior under the influence of drugs and alcohol has led to certain consequences and rejection. It is risky to confront the behavior of chemically dependent people, but to ignore the addiction will only perpetuate the problem. A pastor working with an alcoholic can benefit from attending Al-Anon meetings which follow a twelve-step program for those in relationship with an addict. If you are not familiar with the Twelve Steps, I highly recommend reading the Alcoholics Anonymous (AA) resources that are available at most meetings. Nonalcoholics can attend open meetings. Local meetings are usually listed in the newspaper or can be located by calling the AA number in the phone book. Churches should post easily visible lists of meetings in the area.

Disruption in a survivor's life caused by the psychological complications of addictions and other comorbidities may lead to homelessness, unemployment, bankruptcy, and family breakdown. As stated earlier, addiction must be addressed before any progress can be made with other aspects of chronic PTSD. Once the survivor is in recovery, efforts to regain control over emotions and the ending of self-destructive behaviors will start movement toward healthier interpersonal relationships. The pastor may be called upon to offer spiritual and pastoral guidance to survivors who are confronting guilt and remorse for their behavior when addicted. Recovering addicts may look for assistance in seeking reconciliation with those they have hurt, offended, or alienated. Within twelve-step programs are opportunities for spiritual growth through confession, taking responsibility for hurtful behavior, making restitution for offenses, and asking for forgiveness. In going through this process of self-evaluation and restoration, the recovering addict is likely to experience considerable grief and mourning, especially if relationships remain fractured. The pastor may want to offer a referral to a social worker to help with financial problems and child-custody issues that may exist. The church community may provide a redemptive environment with practical offers of job possibilities and housing options if needed, as well as the spiritual gift of grace—another chance to build connections with people, with God, and with oneself.

CHURCH AS REDEMPTIVE COMMUNITY

Most clergy/rabbis provide pastoral care from the context of a church/synagogue. Pastors should be supported and nurtured by congregations that reflect and mediate God's ongoing redemptive activity in history. People who are members of the congregation, and newcomers who seek compassion and solace, need the environment of a community where they can experience their wholeness. Ideally, a pastor who ministers out of a faith community setting brings an extended network of people offering restoration of connection—a bridge from loneliness and isolation to inclusion and acceptance. When a pastor responds to a pastoral crisis of any kind, the best outreach and support for the long run is as part of a larger group rooted in a spiritual center.

In her book, *Cultivating Wholeness,* Margaret Kornfeld (1998) describes the characteristics of a spiritually centered community that ministers God's grace. These communities "communicate with each other honestly and without fear; resolve conflicts with each other individually and within the group; and learn to love themselves so they can love each other and reach out to strangers. Such communities are safe, inclusive, and just" (p. 19). Creating faith communities of redemption, restoration, and grace requires the leadership, attention, and guidance of a wise and spiritually grounded pastor. Caring for the community, the pastor emphasizes balance, wholeness, spiritual growth, listening, and discernment. Examination of the quality of life in the congregation should be done annually. This assessment should lead to a plan to bring into motion whatever resources are needed to build and sustain a healthy, healing community, welcoming of all those yearning for meaning, affirmation, support, care, and love. All efforts to be a life-affirming, thriving congregation should be celebrated with gratitude. Thankfulness for the opportunity to be cocreators with God will yield hope and joy and reduce anxiety.

A pastor should not be providing pastoral care alone. Putting time and effort into establishing a strong, healing community will assist the pastor, support the spiritually wounded, prevent individual burnout, and provide the means for strengthening the interconnections we share with our secular communities and global partnerships. Every positive change that takes place on a small, local level, contributes to the networking of peace, love, and justice around the world.

Chapter 5

Theological Dimensions
of Spiritual Trauma

We are closer to God when we are asking questions than when we think we have the answers.

Abraham Heschel

Forgiveness is an absolute necessity for continued human existence.

Archbishop Desmond Tutu

THEODICY AND SUFFERING

Spirituality is diverse and difficult to describe fully. Speaking in general terms, spirituality is the part of a person that searches for meaning, purpose, and relationship with others and with the transcendent, the divine, or the higher power. A person's spiritual nature produces qualities such as compassion, forgiveness, love, faith, hope, trust, generosity, and kindness. These characteristics are affected by evil, which produces suffering, leading to the stifling or destruction of some aspect of the spirit. The victim of trauma may feel lost and wounded in some indescribable way that comes across to the observer as anxiety, shame, guilt, loss of control of emotions, weakness, and/or avoidance.

Spiritual trauma may create a crisis of faith. It is not unusual for the victims of trauma to feel that God is punishing them for something they have done. Blaming God as the source of suffering is heard from people who have been grounded in a faith tradition as well as from those who have no previous religious identity of any significance.

There is a general, prevalent religious consensus in Christianity and other major world religions that God is omnipotent and in full control of all events, including the initiation of incidents that bring about suffering to an individual or group. Faith in a God who exercises justice makes experiences of suffering and guilt a problem. This leads to such questions as "Why me?", "What did I do to deserve this?", and "Why is God punishing me?" In the process of exploring these questions and the meaning they hold, the pastor has an essential role as God's ambassador in alleviating suffering and helping survivors to understand their experience in the context of their faith resources.

To be an effective pastoral presence, pastors will need to explore their own theology of suffering and theodicy as it relates to traumatic events. If the pastors believe that God is omnipotent and controls all events, including the imposition of suffering, they will find themselves in the position of having to find justification for the suffering of the righteous, and meaning behind such actions as rape, incest, child abuse, torture, domestic violence, etc. Usually, it is not helpful to say to victims simply that it is not possible for humans to understand God's ways, but that they must humbly accept them until some time in the future when they will understand, i.e., after death or in heaven.

If the pastor also believes that God is trying to discipline or punish someone's behavior through the use of traumatic events, it becomes difficult to avoid taking the position of blaming the victim for what has happened rather than holding the perpetrator accountable. This leads to a retraumatizing of the victim and exacerbates depression, feelings of shame, dirtiness, and worthlessness in God's eyes. These feelings may lead to suicide attempts. It is difficult to see how portraying God as the initiator of suffering can lead to healing in circumstances of severe spiritual trauma. Therefore, it is necessary to explore other explanations for God's role in suffering.

In the biblical traditions, especially the passion narratives, the Psalms, Job, and Lamentations, the question is asked repeatedly, "If God is just, why must the faithful suffer, and the unrighteous ones seem to be unaffected?" Protestant orthodoxy addresses the issue with the belief that God allows evil without supporting it. God will give direction to evil and suffering so that it results in good. Eventually, God will win out over evil. To assert that God allows evil, regardless of the promise of a future, divine, good purpose, remains a stumbling block for victims of traumatic events. The question of the justification of God has been challenged in the aftermath of the Holocaust, Bosnia, apartheid, and modern acts of terrorism such as the bombings in Oklahoma at the Federal Building, the World Trade Center in New York, and most recently culminating in the World Trade Center plane attacks and related events of September 11, 2001.

Probably one of the most helpful approaches is the understanding that God is a covenantal companion with the righteous who suffer, and by God's being in solidarity with those who suffer, they can experience redemption and healing. This approach is different from the belief that suffering should be sought as a form of imitation of Christ's passion. One may freely choose to take a risk and suffer for the sake of bringing about a better situation, but this is very different from suffering that is imposed against one's will. A pastoral response to victims must include a sense of outrage that suffering exists at all, and a reinforcing of God's redeeming purpose to eliminate all suffering, including human participation as cocreators in bringing about the realm of God on earth.

A survivor of incest, Louise M. Garrison has written about her coming to terms with the question "Where was God when I needed God most? . . . the question we ask when there is no more light at the end of the tunnel" (p. 24), in an article titled "Where Was God?" which appeared in *Sojourners,* November 1984. She found her answer in the words of Christ on the cross, *"Eloi, Eloi, lama sabachthani"* ("My God, my God, why have you forsaken me?"). Garrison believes that God demonstrated the final word through the resurrection of Jesus from death. The message of the resurrection is that "coercive power never works; it only destroys: God's final word is Life" (p. 24). God could have chosen to intervene on Good Friday, but this would have required the use of coercive power. Instead, God chose to raise Jesus from the dead, and God is present to raise others to life who are open to the opportunity for new freedom. Each survivor will want to find meaning, will try to make some sense out of his or her trauma. The pastor should be available to support the survivor through what may be a lengthy process.

Clergywomen may be sought out by survivors seeking answers to some of the difficult theodicy questions. Female clergy are sometimes seen as safe, empathic sources of understanding by women who have been traumatized. Here is a case study from my ministry as an example.

One Sunday after worship, while I was greeting people, an unfamiliar young woman came up to me and asked if she could make an appointment to see me in my office. She said she had never heard a female pastor preach before and it sounded to her like I might be able to help her. All I can recall about my sermon was that I preached on a gospel text from Matthew and focused on Jesus and his relationship to Wisdom/Sophia.

Later when we met, the woman (I'll call her Sheila) disclosed to me that she was struggling in psychotherapy to recover from a childhood history of sexual and ritual abuse by three of her brothers and her father. Her family attended church at least twice a week and was immersed in Calvinist theology and the Heidelberg Catechism. Her father was an elder in their church. Although Sheila had confronted her family members and church leadership about her abuse, her pastor did not believe her, and stood firm in supporting her father and brothers in their declaration of innocence. Sheila had believed that her pastor, as a servant of Jesus Christ and the church, would believe her and hold the perpetrators accountable. He did not do so.

Consequently, as a result of her pastor's attitude and the denial of responsibility on the part of her father and brothers, Sheila began to doubt her worthiness in God's eyes. She could make sense of her abuse only by believing that God had been punishing her with sexual abuse to teach her some lesson. Eventually, she sought counseling and her therapist tried to reassure her that God would not do such a thing to anyone. At this point Sheila began to feel that God had abandoned her when he should have been protecting her. Sheila stopped attending church in any denomination for several years and this left her feeling empty because the church and her faith had been the center of her spiritual life.

Sheila said that she had managed to go into a local church about a month ago, and sat in the empty sanctuary, fighting the urge to leave. During that time she had what she described as a "vision" that came to her while she tried to meditate to calm herself. She felt the presence of a female figure who assured her "that everything will be all right." This incident had taken place in my church almost a month before my arrival and it enabled Sheila to sit through a Sunday worship service and to risk speaking to me.

Sheila admitted it was still uncomfortable for her to be speaking about her experience with a pastor, but she said, "I know that the hole inside me will not go away until I deal with my spiritual issues." I realized Sheila had taken a great leap of faith in coming to see me and in disclosing some of the horrific details about her abuse. The ritual abuse had involved the use of candles and animal sacrifice, therefore, language about blood, sacrifice, offering, and the presence of candles could trigger flashbacks.

Sheila's story and spiritual issues highlight several pastoral issues. Survivors such as Sheila need to have their spiritual boundaries respected. They should never be forced into reclaiming their faith or reinitiating church attendance any sooner than they feel ready, and sometimes it takes a very long time to feel comfortable in a religious setting again. Survivors need a pastor who will meet them where they are in their spiritual recovery journey, and accept and support them at their own pace.

Traumatized persons must never be told God was punishing them for their sins or testing their faith. Neither should they be told that the trauma was a spiritual lesson that will teach them to appreciate others' suffering. It is not pastoral to tell them that the experience will strengthen their character or humble them to realize their dependence on God. To make such statements before the victim has processed their way to such an understanding will feel like blame from the victim's perspective and reinflict spiritual wounding.

The comfort and assistance a trauma survivor may need is likely to be practical. Over the next year that I spent providing pastoral support to Sheila, our church helped her pay her rent until state aid came through, a parishioner helped fix her car when it broke down, and I accompanied her to the police and the court house on several occasions as part of her decision to press charges against her father and brothers. Such simple acts hold amazing healing power. Today, Sheila holds a master's degree in clinical mental health counseling and operates her own private practice.

There is no satisfactory, simple answer to theodicy questions. However, at some point in a victim's healing process, he or she may develop an understanding of positive changes in himself or herself as a result of surviving trauma, such as stimulating a deeper quality of compassion. But the evolution to this meaning must not be forced upon the victim. To be supportive, it is necessary for pastors to acknowledge that suffering is real, and that sin and suffering indicate that something is drastically wrong with the world.

As Christian counselors, we can offer victims hope with a radically incarnational theology that sees in the Cross, God's loving, redemptive presence in the midst of suffering and sin and God's effort to eradicate evil in his creation once and for all. No one is alone in his or her suffering for God is with every person, strengthening and guiding him or her to healing and wholeness.

SPIRITUAL CARE AND HEALING

Rather than sounding overly simplistic by quoting scripture about God's love and care (where was God when the abuse was happening?), listen with compassion and empathy and be prepared to listen some more. Most survivors have a need to retell their stories. It is essential that the pastor validate the survivors' emotional reactions and hold the perpetrator(s) responsible for their actions.

Feel free to pray for the survivor privately but always ask first before praying with the person, and speak your prayers aloud.

Try not to be shocked or put off by their anger toward God and resist any urge to defend God. The God revealed to us in scripture is one who can withstand rage and respond with mercy, patience, and compassion.

Remember that the only honest answer to why God let it happen is that we do not know. However, we can make a difference in this person's life now as God's servant by acting in a caring, gentle, compassionate, understanding, nonjudgmental manner. The pastor is a companion through these sometimes overwhelming thoughts. During the crisis stage and beyond, victims of trauma need spiritual care from their faith community, family, and friends, as well as their pastor. People with no background in pastoral care, or those who are uneasy with some of the events that cause spiritual trauma, may be unsure how to respond. But healing takes place in community and is an important part of the process toward recovery and wholeness.

In Harold Kushner's (1981) well-known classic, *When Bad Things Happen to Good People,* he assesses the needs Job expressed and the response he got. This reflection on Job reveals the community's misunderstanding of the support he needed:

> What Job needed from his friends—what he was really asking for when he said, "Why is God doing this to me?"—was not theology, but sympathy. *He did not really want them to explain God to him, and he certainly did not want them to show him where his theology was faulty. He wanted them to tell him that he was in fact a good person, and that the things that were happening to him were terribly tragic and unfair* [italics mine]. But the friends got so bogged down talking about God that they almost forgot about Job, except to tell him that he must have done something pretty awful to deserve this fate at the hands of a righteous God. (p. 86)

This is a good reminder of the kind of sensitivity that is needed from those ministering with the survivor.

At some point, pastors may find the survivor talking about re-venge. This is not the same as righteous anger and the pastor should challenge this need. Revenge can lead to further harm to the victim and it disrupts the justice process. Pastors may find they are the object of displaced anger. It is important to encourage appropriate expres-sion of anger and to assist the survivor in this endeavor.

One of the most useful sources of analysis to help female (and male) trauma survivors direct their anger in an empowering way is found in Beverly Harrison's essay "The Power of Anger in the Work of Love" (Harrison and Robb, 1985). Harrison offers a way for women to overcome the societal gender stereotyping of passivity and use the power behind their anger to effect positive change. Harrison challenges theology that equates spirituality with noninvolvement.

> We do not yet have a moral theology that teaches us the awe-ful, awe-some truth that we have the power through acts of love or lovelessness literally to create one another. . . . The fateful choice is ours, either to set free the power of God's love in the world or to deprive each other of the very basis of person hood and community. (Harrison and Robb, 1985, p. 11)

Harrison goes on to speak about an embodied moral ethic that re-quires respect for all feelings, including anger. To be effective in bringing about change, we must first know what we feel. As survivors of trauma begin to explore the geography of feelings coming to the surface, they will eventually need to find ways to reconnect with other people and the world. Anger can either keep a survivor shut down and alienated from healthy relationships, or when viewed as a signal that something is wrong and a change or transformation is needed, anger can be directed toward social and political endeavors to prevent violence from reoccurring. When we care enough, love enough, to do all we can to stop violence, resistance to evil and allevi-ation of suffering can be seen as radical acts of love not unlike Jesus' crucifixion—the sacrifice he accepted to bring about justice for the marginalized in his culture. Pastors should be prepared to guide and support survivors who choose to become actively involved in trans-forming their anger through antiviolence work in their community, nationally or globally.

FORGIVENESS

One cannot overlook the power of forgiveness in the process of healing. Although, as I have stated previously, forgiveness must not be rushed or demanded of a trauma victim, I doubt that full healing can take place without it. The trauma survivor may have a need to see just punishment of a perpetrator by the legal system and some legitimate sign of repentance on the part of the perpetrator. No one can guarantee that a perpetrator will repent, but salvation is found when repentance meets forgiveness.

Forgiveness is a critical process for reestablishing a right relationship between human beings, and it is a complex process of body, mind, and spirit. Pastors play a role in helping a survivor be in touch with the transcendent, spiritual nature of forgiveness—the soul work that is necessary. For a person to move toward forgiveness, he or she must feel the presence of God as power, energy, or a stimulus working from within herself or himself. It may be possible to deepen one's sense of God's closeness through prayer and meditation that facilitates a relaxation response or a sense of "letting go and letting God" as the Alcoholics Anonymous tradition believes. Breathing exercises can be useful in creating this sense of inner peace, God's comfort, and anxiety reduction as well.

There are similarities between grief work and forgiveness. This connection has been examined by E. Wayne Hill and Paul Mullen in "Contexts for Understanding Forgiveness and Repentance As Discovery: A Pastoral Care Perspective" (2000). They outline the stages as: acknowledging the loss due to injury or injustice; working through the pain of shame and other emotions that precede forgiveness; making adjustments; and transforming the emotional energy of grieving into hopefulness that comes from reconciliation. Emphasis is given to the need to proceed critically and intentionally through each stage.

An illustration of the relationship between grief work and forgiveness can be seen in the story of a woman in her early forties who came to me wrestling with the theology of the commandment to "honor your parents."

Donna's (not her real name) mother was a single parent who raised Donna and her younger sister with minimal assistance in the 1950s. Donna had been physically abused and recalled witnessing her sister being hit until she bled. Donna had also been parentified, and lived within her mother's psychological control until she left home at age twenty-two.

When Donna sought assistance from her pastor, it was at the point that she had entered therapy to grieve the end of a love relationship. During her therapy, she began to recall the childhood abuse at the hands of her mother that she had never dealt with directly. Donna discovered she had forgiven her mother "on an intellectual level" and not from her heart. Our discussions also revealed that Donna's own daughters were about the same age at the time that she was when issues with her mother had reached a crisis point. This may have contributed to the surfacing of Donna's feelings and emotions.

During our meetings, we acknowledged the loss of never having had the mother Donna needed or prayed for. We reflected on how she could "honor" her mother as a person with serious failings, and examine who had fulfilled the mother role or provided a mother image for her during her early years.

Donna became aware of profound feelings of loss, sadness, and anger which she processed with her therapist. I suggested exploring images of God as mother or Goddess, and consider allowing the divine mother to represent the ideal that her human mother could not provide. Donna was also concerned about her own ability to mother her daughters well through adolescence without repeating some of her mother's mistakes. The Mother-God was also a teacher and guide for spiritual parenting, and Donna was disciplined about time spent in prayer, journaling, meditation, and drawing.

Eventually, Donna felt compassion for her mother's unresolved pains and losses that had created barriers to her ability to empathize and express love for her children. In the past, she had argued with her mother about the history of abuse which her mother vehemently denied inflicting. After grieving, expressing her anger, and finding hope in a spirituality of the feminine side of God, Donna felt a new attitude, and let go of the need to have her mother admit to hurting her; she actually no longer dreaded being in her mother's presence.

Donna's forgiveness was as unconditional as God's love. She let go of requiring her mother to take responsibility for her actions and she did not demand an apology. Her feelings of resentment left. Like many of Jesus' teachings such as, "You must lose your life in order to save it," there is a paradox in forgiveness. It appears that the survivor of a traumatic event is being asked to do all the giving, while the perpetrator is the sole benefactor. However, the person who is able to offer the spiritual and moral gift of forgiveness is the one who becomes healed emotionally and spiritually.

If individuals hold on to their anger, pain, hate, and desire for revenge, over time their hearts will harden. As time progresses, each missed opportunity to pursue forgiveness leaves a deepening, calloused scar that becomes less vulnerable to healing. An unhealed wound to the spirit leads to spiritual malaise and a deadened heart. Even when the injury seems too great initially to be able to offer forgiveness, one should at least venture toward healing and open the door to experiencing the transforming power of joy, love, laughter, gratitude, and peace.

In an ideal world, forgiveness and reconciliation would always be preceded by the perpetrator accepting responsibility for his or her be-

...

.....

ibiting repentance, and performing acts of restitution lead-
restoration of balance. Programs such as "Real Justice,"
which originated in the courts of the indigenous people of New Zea-
land, are spreading. Restorative justice addresses the spiritual wounding and presents a forum for open acknowledgment of the perpetrator's responsibility in causing harm. Perpetrators are then freed to
pursue the possibility of restitution and restoration, which frequently
evolves into reconciliation, and an extremely low rate of recidivism.
Real Justice conferencing is based on the social philosophy of partic-
ipatory democracy that affirms and respects the value of every person. The conference facilitator follows a process model that works toward repairing the damage and minimizing any further harm caused
by the offending behavior, and maximizes the social justice achieved
for victims, offenders, and others in the community directly affected
by the event.

PRAYER, MEDITATION, AND HEALING PRACTICES

Chapter 8 discusses the use of ritual to promote spiritual healing.
Contemplative prayer and meditation, as mentioned above, are useful
agents in the healing process. If a pastor does not feel qualified to offer instruction in meditation, it should not be difficult to find someone
who is experienced. A nearby seminary, monastery, Buddhist center,
or some hospitals may offer instruction.

It has been found by monitoring the relaxation response that prayer
and meditation allow a person to feel open to God's presence and actually experience a sense of letting go of bodily tension. Meditation
frequently includes focusing on breathing techniques. Yoga incorporates the benefits of breathing and exercise to create physical and inner harmony. Contemplative prayer is a time of quietness with the an-
ticipation of discovery of one's relationship with God as a beloved
child. The potential to heal shame and other spiritual wounds is infinite. By resting in God's presence and affirming God's love, burdens
may be unloaded. As stated previously, the idea of approaching God
in prayer may not be welcomed by the victim until after any theodicy
issues are addressed.

Other alternative forms of body work such as massage therapy,
Reiki, and polarity therapy may be helpful. Music therapy and holotropic breathwork can also be cleansing experiences. Reiki is an an-

cient healing art that originated in southeast Asia a few thousand years ago. Today's practitioners of Reiki draw upon the teachings of Dr. Mikao Usui, a Christian theologian. The principles of Reiki incorporate both Buddhist and Christian teachings, but they do not adhere to any religious dogma. The healing power of Reiki is based on the belief that there is a universal life force or energy that animates all living things and that this energy can be used for the purpose of healing. A Reiki practitioner channels the energy from his or her upper energy centers through the healer's hands to the recipient. There is no actual physical touch involved. It is believed that in the receiving of the energy, the body's natural ability to heal itself is enhanced. Those persons who have received Reiki treatments report feeling a sensation of warmth or tingling in the area being treated, and an overall sense of relaxation and well-being.

Polarity therapy was developed by Dr. Randolph Stone, a naturopath and an osteopath. Based on the belief that the human body is an energy system with positive, negative, and neutral poles and currents of energy, the polarity therapist seeks to restore balance to the body's cyclic flow of energy by the use of four different approaches: energy work, nutrition, exercise, and counseling. Polarity therapy understands that life energy is the link between the mind and the body.

Music therapy is the use of music by a qualified person to bring about positive changes in the psychological, physical, cognitive, or social functioning of individuals with health or educational problems. Music therapy has proven successful in treating substance abuse problems, and acute and chronic pain.

A music therapist makes an assessment of the patient's needs and designs music sessions that may include music and imagery, receptive music listening, song writing, music improvisation, and performance. Healthy individuals can benefit from music to reduce stress through passive listening for relaxation or active music making, such as drumming.

Holotropic breathwork is the trademark breathing technique developed in the mid-1970s by Stanislav Grof, MD, and his wife Christina Grof. Holotropic is derived from the Greek; it means moving toward wholeness. The holotropic breathwork technique involves the use of evocative, rhythmic music, a partner who sits and observes the breathing session, art, focused energy release work, and usually group sharing to integrate the experience. The entire session is supervised by a certified facilitator who provides information about non-ordinary states of consciousness before participation. Through the use of controlled breathing, beginning with hyperventilation, the body enters a state where the goals of wholeness, healing, and wisdom may be met. Holotropic breathwork operates under the principle that we each possess our own inner healer that can best be accessed to do its work in a nonordinary state of consciousness.

Many treatments such as these have been labeled "New Age" and are considered taboo in Christian circles, but they have been known to assist people in accessing wounds that have been resistant to talk therapy alone. It is advisable to support survivors who find success with these therapies, and it is helpful for pastors to know of reputable providers in their region.

Native Americans also have dynamic, spiritual healing resources available to them through their shamans and medicine men who guide them through the use of herbs and rituals. Pastors should honor these traditions alongside the Christian beliefs a native person may espouse.

God will see to it that our wounds do not get the best of us. Through the passionate power of divine compassion in its diverse and numerous forms, healing happens.

Chapter 6

Special Needs and Issues of Veterans

When tears come, I breathe deeply and rest. I know I am swimming in a hallowed stream where many have gone before. I am not alone, crazy, or having a nervous breakdown. . . . My heart is at work. My soul is awake.

Mary Margaret Funk

Combat veterans, POWs, and those wounded in action endure trauma physically, psychologically, and spiritually. Exposure to death and suffering is immense. Psychological breakdown in combat during World War II was 300 percent greater than in World War I. During the Korean War, clinicians were present to offer immediate, on-site treatment with the hope the soldier would return to duty as soon as possible. Battlefield psychological breakdown in the Vietnam War was low compared to previous wars, as a result of the preventive measures initiated in Korea. However, as the war progressed, it became clear that the phenomenon documented during World War II, but considered rare, was being experienced in some soldiers suffering from acute combat reactions, as well as in colleagues who had no symptoms at the end of the war. These common symptoms included nightmares of battle, rage and aggressive behavior, extreme anxiety, depression, and problems with relationships. As the war began to wind down in the 1970s, the number of veterans manifesting psychiatric disorders began to increase at a rapid rate (Goodwin, 1981).

Other mental health personnel working with survivors of various traumatic episodes during the early 1970s such as terrorism, plane crashes, and natural disasters began to recognize that many of the victims of these traumatic experiences had symptoms similar to those of the Vietnam veterans. After years of research, the DSM-III published in 1980 included a new category: post-traumatic stress disorder.

Many factors contribute to the large numbers of Vietnam veterans afflicted with PTSD. The average age of Vietnam combatants was nineteen, a time in adolescent psychological development when individuals are usually establishing a more concrete sense of self and strengthening their adult personality. This process was disrupted and contributed to readjustment and identity problems for young veterans. Comorbidities, such as drug and alcohol abuse in Vietnam veterans, stem from the sanctioned use of drugs by the U.S. military. "Amphetamines were used to promote wakefulness. Alcohol was used extensively, and was commonly provided to units following actions or deployment. Phenothiazines and other tranquilizers were also used for the first time in combat" (Jones, 1975, p. 17). The widespread use of marijuana served a purpose in that it "muted the stress of combat and repressed fear, guilt, and grief (Horowitz, 1975)" (Blair and Hildreth, 1991, p. 17).

Vietnam was primarily fought as a guerrilla war. The enemy was difficult to identify and frequently included civilians, women, or the elderly—those whom American males are traditionally raised to defend. The Vietnam War also sent home far higher rates of survivors who were disabled or wounded than did World War II and Korea. In addition to posttraumatic symptoms, Vietnam veterans were victims of unique, situational conditions that contributed to obstacles upon reentry to society.

War devastates the soul. Many recruits comment that the spiritual trauma began in boot camp where they experienced personally, or witnessed, brutality to the point of killing. Others were subjected to loss of dignity and a devaluing of human life (Barton and LaPierre, 1999). One Vietnam veteran described his soul as having been "burned to a crisp" (Kuenning, 1991). It is most disturbing for Vietnam veterans to look back on their experiences and acknowledge that they broke moral commandments with few or no second thoughts at the time. They sometimes found themselves "enjoying" or seeking the thrill of killing as a means of relief from the overwhelming stress (Barton and LaPierre, 1999). Some veterans, who later on began to process their actions, recognized that they had violated God's commandments by raping Vietnamese women, killing people and encouraging killing and other heinous acts, drinking alcohol to excess, and using illegal drugs. Many felt that God would not forgive what they had done and feared God would want to punish them.

It is not unusual for me to make a pastoral hospital visit as a VA chaplain with a Vietnam veteran who quickly warns me not to start speaking about "how what I did 'in country' was okay, because it was during wartime and I was just doing my duty. It doesn't matter why I did it. It was wrong. Killing is wrong." Occasionally, the veteran will go on to describe in detail what he did. The most unsettling actions are the killing of women and children, accidentally or intentionally, and physical acts of torture performed while the victim was still alive. I believe that through the process of speaking or "confessing" these acts to a chaplain, who does not get up and leave or condemn or rationalize them, the veteran is given an opportunity to confront the feelings he has about his behavior that he has repressed. Guilt haunts the veteran's spiritual life as well as fear of God's wrath. The veteran may also be angry with God for allowing the horrific events of war to happen. When the veteran is hospitalized and possibly facing a life-threatening illness, he may also fear "going to hell" when he dies. A combat veteran may feel powerless to make amends for his actions and may see himself as an unforgivable participant in evil activity.

The belief that God's mercy does not apply to a veteran's actions creates alienation and isolation from God. Some veterans continue to experience lack of control over their urges to commit violence, and find themselves attracted to the feeling of power and control when they are violent. The social and relational consequences of violent behavior contributes to a growing sense of loneliness. The possibility of reclaiming their spiritual base and reconnection with God seems out of reach. Despair and hopelessness threaten their souls. The spiritual dimension of the trauma runs deep. The extent of spiritual loss may feel overwhelming and beyond recovery.

One Vietnam combat veteran, who served for three years during the Tet Offensive, needed to talk about his experience when he was admitted for a life-threatening illness. His recollection of the most disturbing aspect of his time in Vietnam is a revealing overview of several themes that I hear often as a VA chaplain.

> I was seventeen when I killed my first human, and many died around me. It's a feeling that never leaves you. You never get over seeing your friends die. . . . I sometimes wish I'd left a part of me there, but I guess I did when I think of my scars. They gave me Benzedrine—I didn't know what it was at the time—to keep me awake so I could go on fighting. I just thought it would

help me cope and stay awake, but I came home addicted. . . .The "gooks"—I try not to use that word anymore—were no different than us, but we were never allowed to call them Vietnamese. Anything else, but not Vietnamese, that would make them human. We were supposed to see them as less than human. . . . Sometimes I wake up at 1:30 in the morning on the kitchen floor in my Skivvies with the police knocking at my door. I don't remember it, but while in a flashback, I've called 911 asking for help: "I'm surrounded and need another squadron up here!" The police came with four cars the first time. Now they understand what happens to me, and they just come and talk. . . . I'm really angry at the politicians who traded lives for money.

Pastors know Vietnam veterans because they are members of their church and/or community. It is possible that they attend church or have wives and/or children who attend church. Frequently, the pastor is called upon to assist with a pastoral need in the family that may be connected to the problems arising from PTSD and related spiritual issues. Pastoral care with Vietnam veterans in particular requires sensitivity and awareness. Veterans may have spiritual wounds that have eroded their capacity to trust, especially in authority figures. A pastor, viewed as God's representative, may not be well-received. The pastor becomes a reminder of their loss of connection with God and their spirituality. Nevertheless, the fact that clergy do represent a possible source for reconnection with God, or at the least a person with whom to discuss spiritual issues, provides an opportunity to offer the living reminder of God's compassion by accepting veterans in the midst of their doubt, cynicism, and self-loathing.

The pastor may be a source of hope for healing and transformation. As a spiritual guide, the pastor may have the opportunity to point out that by accepting responsibility for their actions in wartime, they have taken an important initial step in the Christian approach to spiritual healing. Next is the desire to reestablish a right relationship with God. In order to move toward self-respect once again, a right relationship with God comes first. A pastor may be a spiritual companion for the grief process associated with a veteran's spiritual recovery process.

Veterans sustain the devastating loss of their comrades and an overwhelming list of other incalculable losses. The grieving process has a primary role in spiritual healing because of these losses: loss of faith in God/religion, government, and authority; loss of intimate relationships; loss of ability to express compassion and empathy; loss of job and home; loss of hope in the future; loss of ability to experience joy, laughter, and fun; and loss of self-worth and self-esteem. Giving a veteran permission and a safe space to grieve is an act of pastoral outreach. Acknowledging the church's and society's contributions to the negative postwar environment for veterans may be helpful, but it is usually nonjudgmental listening that conveys patience and caring, which is fundamental for establishing trust.

The ideal situation would be for the veteran to seek assistance from the nearest veterans administration hospital. VA hospitals have PTSD recovery programs, vet centers, and veterans' support groups. Most facilities will have chaplains familiar with the spiritual issues present in PTSD who can assist veterans and their pastors in creating a partnership for the healing journey. To find the nearest vet center, check your local phone directory under United States Government and Veterans Administration. You may also want to contact the local veterans' organization and get to know who the veterans are in your area who would be willing to speak to your congregation.

Pastors should keep in mind the questions that are likely to arise from the veterans' experience, and be prepared by having conducted their own theological reflection, especially if they never served in the military themselves. Veterans may wrestle with such spiritual questions as: Where was God in Vietnam? Does doing evil ever lead to accomplishing good? Is it OK to hate God? Why does God allow war? How can God forgive the horrible things I have done?

Some Vietnam veterans with prolonged PTSD and comorbidities have worked against great odds toward rekindling their spiritual growth and development. I have heard the stories of veterans who killed civilian women and children and continue to suffer from occasional flashbacks and nightmares, yet they are committed to some symbol of restitution. One veteran told me of his missionary work in Nicaragua, teaching children how to draw and paint, creating vibrant colored murals for the walls of restored schools. Many veterans realize it is not possible to go directly to the Vietnamese and tell them they are sorry for the killings, but by reaching out to other needy children in a war-torn country, they are redeeming their past and showing themselves and others that they can be kind, moral, and caring people.

I have had veterans report to me being disappointed and disillusioned by responses from clergy with whom they have consulted. The needs of veterans are unique; pastors should make an effort to gain an understanding of post-traumatic stress disorder and become educated about what is helpful for veterans. There are some specific comments that should be avoided. Never tell veterans you know what they have been through. Even if you have served in the military, your experiences were different. Veterans need you to be willing to listen, but if they choose not to talk about the war, this must be respected as well. Never tell a veteran it is time to put the war behind him and get on with his life. He is likely to resent it, and the war experience will always be a part of his life. Avoid sharing your political views about the war unless the veteran specifically asks you. The veteran needs to be the one doing the talking and he is likely to shut down if he feels you are judging him. Even if a veteran is angry with the government about the war, it is likely that he is still proud of serving his country and remains strongly patriotic.

The foremost issue for postcombat PTSD is trust. According to Robert Rosenheck, Director of the Veterans Affairs Medical Center, Northeast Program Evaluation Center, West Haven, Connecticut, successful treatment of PTSD must prioritize addressing substance abuse, then treatment of depression, anxiety, and obsessive-compulsive disorder. A person who wishes to be supportive to veterans with PTSD should "project a positive and optimistic attitude," remembering that the Vietnam veterans "have been demoralized" (videotape, VA National Center for PTSD, 1997).

Operation Desert Storm (ODS), the U.S. military invasion of Iraq in 1991, appears to have resulted in far fewer cases of combat-related PTSD. Veterans of ODS received support from their families. The mass media and politicians were less critical of this invasion than of Vietnam. Communities welcomed their veterans home and offered a positive environment for debriefing and readjusting. Nevertheless, for those who do suffer from PTSD after ODS, it will remain important not to discount their experiences with dismissive remarks about it being only a 100-hour war with very few casualties. It is not unusual for PTSD to have late onset twenty to fifty years after exposure to the trauma when the veteran is faced with other stressors such as divorce or retirement.

New approaches to the treatment of PTSD such as EMDR (eye movement desensitization and reprocessing), incident reduction, EKP (emotional kinesthetic psychotherapy), and thought-field therapy have provided sufferers of chronic symptoms with hope for lasting resolution. Supportive pastors should be aware of the local availability of the latest treatments in order to direct people to these resources.

FEMALE VETERANS

Before the creation of the Vietnam Women's Memorial, there were 110 monuments in Washington, DC, and not one depicted women in the military, although women have served in all of America's wars. Exact figures for the number of women who served in Vietnam are difficult to obtain because the government did not keep close count:

> The most commonly accepted figures are that, of an estimated 250,000 women who served our country during the Vietnam era (1964-1975), 10,000 women, both military and civilian, are believed to have served in Vietnam. Ninety percent of the women who were there were nurses. (Kuenning, 1991, p. 74)

The average age of the women in Vietnam was twenty-five. Most of the women had volunteered. Many of the stressors faced by women in a combat zone were similar to those experienced by other soldiers, but there were significant differences, some of which were gender related. The military had been reluctant to deploy women to Southeast Asia because of concern for how they would respond in a combat zone or any place that had undesirable climate, facilities, or working conditions. According to retired USAF Major General Jeanne Holm (1992) in her book *Women in the Military,* there was an attitude of overprotectiveness "based on the notion that the women would not be able to cope with the slightest inconvenience without loss of morale and efficiency. . . . Applying similar criteria to men would never have occurred to anyone" (p. 224).

Research evaluating the stressors on women who served in the Vietnam war zone is minimal. In 1990, the National Vietnam Veterans Readjustment Study (NVVRS) (Kulka, 1990) included data from 296 women veterans. The NVVRS substantiated the findings of three earlier small-scale studies. The evidence is conclusive that women veterans exposed to war-zone stress are likely to develop symptoms that interfere with their ability to function in everyday life.

"Stressors ranked highest by the women included nursing duties and responsibilities, witnessing the mutilation of young bodies, negating their emotions, and supply shortages" (Furey, 1991, p. 12).

The injuries and casualties in Vietnam were predominantly the result of guerrilla warfare that involved the use of small arms: "booby traps, punji sticks, claymore mines, high velocity bullets. Nearly all inflict multiple wounds of the most vicious mutilating kind" (Drake, 1967, p. 75). Sometimes nurses and other health care personnel would be under attack during surgical procedures:

> if the attack was bad, we would lower the operating tables as low as possible so we could operate on our knees, but you had to keep going and you did. . . . We had several guys come in with live grenades still in their bellies. We operated with sand bags around the table. If you allowed your own fears to show through, you could lose the person in front of you on the operating table. You couldn't do that, so you blocked it out." (Holm, 1992, p. 233)

The number of injured who survived as a result of such dedication and service is amazing. "Less than two percent of the casualties treated died as a result of their wounds" (Holm, 1992, p. 233).

Even though nurses did all they could to save lives, some patients did die and the nurses in those cases experienced feelings of guilt and helplessness. Another area in which nurses made a significant contribution was toward the upkeep of morale. Expectations in this regard, however, also involved expectations to participate in parties outside of the confines of the unit. A nurse who refused to attend could be judged as unpatriotic. Some nurses have reported "failure to comply, indeed attempts to 'buck the system' on any issue, resulted in transfer to more dangerous locations, denial of 'R and R' or changes in duty schedule" (Kuenning, 1991, p. 76). Northwestern State University conducted a study in 1984 that documented the added stress resulting from reported sexual harassment that included rape and assault, insults, unwanted attention, and sexist remarks.

When women came home from Vietnam, they too were subjected to degrading remarks such as "whore" and "baby killer." Unknown numbers of women veterans have committed suicide since the war. Many continue to live with the effects of PTSD and only recently have their issues been addressed by the establishment of special women's programs within the VA, such as the Center for Women Veterans and its satellite services designed to be responsive to the gender-specific needs of women veterans.

Since the Vietnam era, women have served in the military in increasing numbers. Currently, 14 percent of U.S. active-duty military forces are women and some 1.2 million women are military veterans. Post-Vietnam U.S. involvement in major combat situations has been limited to the Gulf War's Operation Desert Storm where 35,000 women served. Over 1,000 women participated in U.S. military operations in Somalia between 1992 and 1994 based on Defense Manpower Data Center statistics. In 1995, over 1,200 women served in Operation Uphold/Support Democracy in Haiti, and over 5,000 have been deployed with the United Nations' forces in Operation Joint Endeavor to Bosnia. Women in the military continue to be subjected to sexual harassment and sexual violence while they are stationed throughout the world.

Sometimes female soldiers feel guilty about not being able to defend themselves against a sexual assault. It is common for members of her professional and social network to blame the female soldier as they try to rationalize an event such as rape. For the victim, it is likely that she has been violated by someone who was once a source of camaraderie. Thus, someone whom she may have counted on has become a threat. A female soldier, regardless of her rank, is subjected to the effects of a dominant patriarchal system that is sustained by traditional gender roles and cultural expectations surrounding female behavior. My experience with female veterans who are also married to enlisted men indicates there is an increased incidence of domestic violence as well. What we are likely seeing is the social and spiritual consequence of training people to kill.

GENDER ISSUES AND SPIRITUALITY

The spiritual issues for women veterans are not unlike those of civilian women and are related to the social and cultural issues of gender. In one of the spirituality groups that I co-led for female veterans with PTSD resulting from sexual trauma, the question of God's apparent lack of protection and intervention was asked repeatedly. Some had trouble with the male image of God. Many of the women had struggled to overcome the shame of rape and the associated self-concept of being "dirty" and "unworthy." Self-blame held weight over any responsibility they initially gave the perpetrator. Some of the women had trouble convincing their senior officers that a crime had been committed against them. These women have encountered in the military what is also true in our North American white culture. Male power and dominance acts as a filter for most women's spirituality and experience. Women's ways of knowing, being, and experiencing are frequently called into question, dismissed, and silenced, contributing to the intensification of posttrauma stress and unconscious anger and rage.

Culture and society requires and influences female personalities to follow along gender lines. The prescribed roles and behavior for women that are acceptable condition women for becoming victims. When women's behavior crosses into the traditional area of male roles and power, most women will experience anxiety and stress as they attempt to expand their personal agency. Conflicts are likely to arise intrapersonally and interpersonally when women move out of their gender roles, for example: from helplessness to self-determination; from inferior and unintelligent to intellectual and articulate; from subordinate/passive/compliant to assertive and resistant; from the seductive "bad girl" to a sense of sacred embodiment, self-pleasure, and woman identification; from fearful to courageous/risk taker (by choice); from emotional/hysterical to valuing, trusting of feelings and intuition; from predominantly sensitive to others' needs to knowing oneself; from the "nice girl" who is always happy and cooperative to expressing anger; from obedience and doing as instructed to original thinking and expressions of creativity; from dependency and the subject of control and possession to being an empowered, free individual; from being primarily a giver who serves others to being a receiver; from upholding traditional expectations to changing and progressing; from meeting everyone's needs as a "super-woman" to drawing boundaries and saying "no"; from being a wife and mother to choosing to be single and childless, or honoring one's sexual orientation as a lesbian. Whenever a woman steps outside of her culture's role expectations, she is likely to suffer resistance and attempts from both male and female keepers of the power structure to prevent her from deviating from the established norms of behavior. However, many women who live under the prescribed roles experience depression, loss of self, loss of affiliation with their spiritual center, and alienation from God.

Depending on one's childhood religious participation and its lingering influence, a person with PTSD may have more or less difficulty in dealing with the spiritual issues of trauma. Women who seek pastoral counseling concerning their religious and spiritual issues may benefit from exposure to alternatives to the spirituality and theology they learned in traditional religious settings. Pastors should be able to teach a woman-affirming spirituality that offers concepts and images that give women an opportunity to discover and explore the feminine face of God. Scripture is abundant with female images of God that are rarely read or discussed in church. Recent biblical scholarship and the scriptural interpretations of contemporary feminist liberation theologians have brought to light an alternative imaging of God and many other biblical figures that affirm women's roles in the ongoing story of creation and redemption (see Chapter 9 for resources).

If a pastor or chaplain is working with a female survivor of trauma individually or in a group, it is useful to encourage the woman to write her spiritual autobiography. This is also something the pastor should have done and, if not, pastors should write one and when the time is appropriate in the group or with the individual, share their story. A spiritual autobiography highlights key experiences and decisions which persons have made in their lifetime concerning their faith and spirituality. The writing process allows the person to clarify his or her history of religious beliefs and practices and to reflect on how this has influenced his or her current beliefs. With guidance from the pastor, relevant theological themes and existential issues can be highlighted for discussion. Issues of spiritual wounding are likely to come to the surface where they can be dealt with. This is where the theological issues of theodicy, suffering, and evil will arise. Additional issues such as guilt, shame, self-blame, and forgiveness also frequently emerge at this time.

When survivors are able to reclaim their spirituality as a source of healing and empowerment, they develop a renewed sense of hope and a more realistic and balanced view of the world. Discovering new pathways to express their evolving beliefs, while reconnecting with their religious roots, may provide a trauma survivor with meaning and comfort.

Chapter 7

Pastoral Care Issues
for the Pastor/Caregiver

At our best, we become Sabbath for one another. We are the emptiness, the day of rest. We become space, that our loved one, the lost and the sorrowful may find rest in us.

Wayne Muller

ROLE OF THE PASTOR

For pastors to be helpful in supporting someone with PTSD, it is required that they have some basic skills in pastoral care in addition to a thorough understanding of the disorder and the ways it impacts one's life. As in any situation calling for a pastoral response, it is essential that the pastor be a spiritually grounded person in regular contact with a spiritual director, pastoral supervisor, or other mentor. These contacts provide an opportunity for growth in the pastor's own understanding of spiritual leadership, and provide a way for processing personal issues that may arise when involved with intense pastoral situations.

Pastors have a responsibility to those who turn to them for pastoral care to maintain clear boundaries, to acknowledge their limitations and make appropriate referrals, and to have spent time reflecting on and developing their theology of evil, suffering, healing, and salvation. In particular, a pastor's theology could deepen the spiritual wounds of trauma if it leads to blaming the victim. It is essential that pastors receive education from professionals with a dual background in theological studies and pastoral counseling in cases of trauma, so that they may facilitate spiritual healing and wholeness.

Reflection on Theology of Evil, Suffering, Healing, and Salvation

The Hebrew scriptures typically portray Yahweh (God) as the one who gives both illness and healing, with illness depicted as the result of disobedience or sin. Some examples of this can be found in the following scriptural verses:

> Sickness—Leviticus 26:14-16; Numbers 12:9-15; Deuteronomy 28:20-22 ff.; 1 Samuel 5:6-12; 2 Kings 5:27; Job 5:17-18; Psalm 38:1-8; Isaiah 10:16; Hosea 5:13-6:2
> Healing—Exodus 15:26; Deuteronomy 7:15; Job 5:17-18; Psalm 41:3-4; 107:17-20; Jeremiah 30:17; Hosea 5:13-6:2
> Result of sin—Leviticus 26:14-16; Psalm 38:1-8; 41:3-4; 107:17-20

Theology that blames the victims for their illness is a challenge for pastors who minister to those with any kind of sickness, and it is important to wrestle with defining a pastoral response to people who believe God is punishing them for their behavior.

The Christian scriptures identify healing as central to the public ministry of Jesus Christ. The Gospel stories are a rich source for those who seek to find meaning in their suffering and wholeness in the midst of chronic limitations. Jesus' recorded healings and exorcisms also make it clear that not all sickness is the result of sin. It is beyond the scope of this book to develop a theology of evil, suffering, healing, and salvation, but in essence, pastors should realize that all influences that seek to obstruct wellness and spiritual growth are in contradiction to God's will, which constantly seeks restoration of the people. (For some excellent resources on this topic, see the bibliography.)

Personal Psychological History

The human ability to be sensitive to someone's circumstances, their feelings, their afflictions, and deep levels of compassion are usually the result of having had a similar personal experience our self. We understand someone else better the closer our own experiences parallel theirs. Although this blesses us with the benefits of the feeling of kinship, we are also at risk for transference and projection.

Pastors should be aware of the dynamics of transference and projection so that they can grace their parishioners with compassion, but avoid having their personal experiences negatively influence the process and the self-discovery, which belongs uniquely to the parishioner. Transference occurs when the pastor's repressed or forgotten emotions about a past event are shifted from the original source of the feelings to the person the pastor is currently dealing with. Projection is the process or result of externalizing or objectifying a perception or mental image and assigning it to another person as though it were their own.

As one might imagine from these brief definitions, transference and projection can lead to confusion and complications in the pastoral relationship. However, when one is aware of what one is doing, and acts to stop these behaviors, once again the value of shared experiences to promote healing is immeasurable.

Offering Support

By becoming knowledgeable about PTSD and its symptoms and causes, pastors are less likely to be shocked by the stories they will hear from those who have been traumatized. It is important not to appear repulsed by the victims' descriptions and their need to retell the event to you several times over. This is part of their process of gaining your trust and evaluating your willingness to acknowledge their experience as real as they know it. This is when it is important to validate the wrongness of what the perpetrator did and hold the perpetrator responsible for the trauma. Avoid making patronizing statements such as "I understand" or "I know what you mean." No one has had exactly the same experience, and to say otherwise diminishes the significance of the victims' suffering.

Compassion

Compassionate response is quite often simply a matter of listening well and guiding the person in finding an appropriate counseling referral or other local community resources. Pastors have a responsibility to identify these resources early on in their ministry and, if at all possible, meet with the professionals and establish connections.

Being available to pray with a victim or survivor and to discuss the religious and spiritual questions that are likely to arise is an essential component to the pastor's role. Entering a partnership with the person that supports him or her through therapy and provides a safe place to explore questions is symbolic of many biblical characters whose relationships helped them to make it through a difficult journey, such as Ruth and Naomi, David and Jonathan, Aaron and Moses, Jesus and the disciples, Paul and Silas, and many more.

Simply being present for the expression of pain is an act of healing. I have found the Buddhist practice of "presence and detachment" valuable in many aspects of pastoral ministry. Learning this spiritual discipline enables a pastoral caregiver to be an intimate listener and to express compassion without becoming overinvolved, or stressed to the point of burnout.

Presence and Detachment

Good listening skills are a fundamental tool for compassionate pastoral care. Pastors who are good listeners have the quality of being in the moment with a person. This ability to be fully present is much more than just being there physically and making eye contact. It involves the pastor's full concentration on what is being spoken and it requires an open heart.

I had a theology professor at seminary who was in great demand because of her wisdom and compassion. She was always surrounded by students waiting to have a discussion with her. This woman was a model for me of undisturbed presence. In spite of the many people lined up needing to speak with her, whenever I approached her, she had the ability to convey the sense that the rest of the world was blocked out at that moment, and the only two people in the room at that time were the two of us. She was fully engaged, undistracted, unrushed, and calm. Each person received her full attention. It has been my goal to strive to nurture that same sense of totally concentrating on the other person and his or her communication with me.

Presence is more a matter of being than doing. Most of the time as pastors we are observers. We offer people a safe space to be simply who they are and respected for who they are without judgment. By accepting and witnessing someone's darkest fears or behavior, we allow them to accept themselves. We create a healing environment by letting the Spirit of God permeate the time we spend together, and avoid hindering the process with an awkward need to say or do the "right" thing.

Detachment is related to the art of presence. In order that we can be free to move on to the next person or activity that calls for our attention, pastors also benefit from the Buddhist concept of "detachment." Before I fully understood this concept, I was turned off by what sounded like uncaring or abandonment. Now, to me, detachment is a kind of letting go after a moment of compassion or empathy, when a pastor has experienced deep sharing and profound vulnerability. Detachment allows the pastor to leave the issue or the problem with the person after having embraced it together. Healing belongs to the individual and we steal their healing potential if we get so overinvolved and wrapped up in our desire to help or fix the problem that we try to do their work for them. We cannot take the journey for them, we can only walk alongside.

GENDER ISSUES AND SEXUALITY

If the goal of pastoral care and support is to guide people to wholeness through a spiritual journey, then pastors should be conscious of gender issues that may arise. Especially when ministering with women, white, Western cultural stereotypes should be avoided. A woman who has been victimized by a male perpetrator does not need a male pastor reminding her of traditional, subservient, female marital roles when she is attempting to recover from domestic violence or marital rape. It is imperative that all pastors become informed of nontraditional, scholarly, biblical interpretations of the passages that are frequently used to rationalize keeping women in abusive relationships.

Female pastors who are unfamiliar with theologies that can liberate men from the dominator role should also seek counsel and education. If female pastors find themselves trapped with a stereotype that all men abuse power in relationships, they may not be able to practice presence and compassion toward a male victim. When I encountered my first case of domestic violence in a family of active church members, I was approached by the woman who was being threatened and beaten by her husband. I knew both of them, but was not able to offer pastoral care to both partners, even individually. I had not done enough reading or listening to perpetrators to have the understanding necessary to be compassionate and helpful to them. I did give the husband a referral to an agency that worked with batterers. However, I slowly came to realize that these men had stories as well and for me to minister to their issues around power and a history of violence in their lives, I needed to address my own feelings of judgment toward perpetrators of violence.

Although I continue to avoid working with both the victim and the perpetrator at the same time, I can now hear and be present for the men as well. I have discovered that when a male perpetrator seeks pastoral care from a female pastor or chaplain, the clergywoman must be very savvy about potential manipulation and her level of vulnerability. However, I have also seen men benefit from the authority of the female pastorate when it is used to hold them accountable for their behavior while also offering them a process for reclaiming self-respect and their personhood. Guiding them through a spiritual journey that reflects on authority, power, and control may lead toward a desire for personal change and an offer of restitution to the victim. This is usually a lengthy process and requires that the perpetrator also be active in a counseling program for violent offenders. There are numerous erudite publications on male spirituality that can enlighten and inform clergymen and clergywomen of men's spiritual struggles in a patriarchal culture.

The millions of men who have been victims of childhood sexual abuse have little room in our culture for processing their grief, shame, and issues such as trust, intimacy, and sexuality. Men are expected to be able to protect themselves in any situation and to be able to handle any problem on their own. The kind of macho attitude that encourages men to take revenge and then forget about it has left many adult male survivors with unresolved feelings of anger, confusion, and self-doubt regarding their manhood. Pastors who are working with adult male survivors will benefit greatly from Mike Lew's (1990) book *Victims No Longer,* which specifically addresses the issues that men face in their healing journey. Helping men recognize what they have been taught about power and masculinity, and how that conditioning affects their acknowledgment of abuse and their recovery, will contribute to their self-understanding and possibly alleviate some of their self-blame. To offer this kind of support, pastors must have a critique of our patriarchal culture (see Chapter 12).

Whenever trauma has been experienced, it is likely that other issues and struggles that were present in the person's life at the time will continue to impact the healing process in some way. Pastors should not make assumptions about a person's sexuality, particularly if the person is not well known to them. Unfortunately in our society, it is not unusual for a gay, lesbian, bisexual, or transgendered person to become a victim of a violent act. Sometimes, a nonheterosexual person will feel ashamed and guilt-ridden that their sexual orientation in some way caused the violence. Self-blaming may not be directly and openly expressed to the pastor out of fear of further recrimination. There may be vague references to being a "bad person in God's eyes" or "deserving of what I got because of who I am." Pastors should be prepared when it appears that sexuality issues are coming to the surface.

Once again, it will be necessary for the pastor to explore personal issues surrounding sexual identity and the human sexual spectrum. Especially in the aftermath of a traumatic event is no time for a pastor to discuss sexual orientation issues in a negative way. Should a pastor feel ambivalent or abhorrent toward gay, lesbian, bisexual, or transgendered persons, it is essential for the minister to seek balance in his or her theology by exposure to other religious viewpoints with an open mind. If the pastor's prejudices about sexual identity, or any other issue for that matter, appear to be impeding the pastoral relationship, it may be best for the pastor to refer the person to someone else to assist in healing the spiritual wound.

RACE, CLASS, AND CULTURAL ISSUES

Other issues that affect a person's ability to pastor in any pastoral situation are race, class, and multiculturalism. Racial stereotypes still abound in all parts of our country, and even well-meaning pastors may be unaware of ingrained racist attitudes and assumptions that can influence the pastoral relationship. Any pastor who has not been personally challenged to explore his or her internalized racism should be counseled on this issue before ministering with a person of a different race.

It is also possible that a pastor will overlook culturally based issues that may be of importance to a person's healing process. For example, pastoral care with African-American women that is based on traditional pastoral care paradigms may assume that because an African-American woman has demonstrated persistence, courage, and strength in her life, she may be discounted as having little, if any, need for pastoral care other than simple compassion. Those pastors with a broader understanding of the complexity of an African-American woman's self-concept and familial roles will be better prepared to listen to her proclamation of faith and hear it as both a source of spiritual strength and a pastoral need.

Pastoral caregivers also tend to place great value in vulnerability as a contributing factor to the healing process. It will be risky for a woman of color to access her vulnerability when, outside the context of pastoral care, she is struggling with social and political prejudices. Women of color are grounded in their communities and will feel a responsibility to others where they have their sense of belonging. All of these characteristics of nonwhite culture, and many more I have not mentioned, contribute to the formation of theology and spirituality of people of color. A pastoral caregiver must be committed to learning what a person means by their faith statements, and how they make use of these beliefs and meanings. Each culture will make a unique contribution to a person's faith development. The pastor can facilitate healing by "assisting . . . in a process of meaning-making and reflecting on the elements of the faith system . . . examined for meaning and application but also critiqued for their contradiction with the womanist's actual life experiences" (Snorton, 1996, p. 63).

Generally speaking, churches have been more silent about covert prejudice based on issues of class. Pastors should be conscious of the impact of economic oppression. Class differences create power imbalances and subject people to restrictions in access to quality health care and education when they live at the lower end of the class hierarchy. There may be a need for victims to claim their voices and regain their languages of expression before they will be able to describe the full meaning of their experiences and see their way toward healing. It may take some time devoted to identifying and naming their spiritual strengths. The devaluing and eroding of personal value and self-esteem is a a core mechanism of the disempowerment of classism. When pastors are making referrals to mental health counselors and health care providers, it may require advocacy with the person for access to the full range of resources.

It is crucial to be aware of the paternalism and maternalism that well-meaning pastors may project when working with people of a lower class status than themselves. People are capable of making choices and taking action when they are given adequate information. Support, advocacy, guidance, and other kinds of "help" from the pastor should always seek to enable the person's autonomy and self-determination.

ALTERNATIVE SPIRITUALITY

Usually, pastors are providing pastoral care from the Judeo-Christian tradition. The spiritual resources identified by Christian religious teachings may not be sufficient for individuals depending on their own spiritual growth and developmental stage, their ethnic and cultural background, and if they have had negative past experiences with clergy and organized religion. Persons seeking healing and recovery from trauma, particularly if the trauma was in any way connected to religious leadership or religious ritual, may be involved with, or curious about, spiritual practices outside their usual frame of reference. Pastors need to assess for themselves what they are willing to recommend, introduce, and support outside their own spiritual practices, and consider the need to direct a person to the spiritual support systems and practices they need.

For example, it is not unusual for a Native American who has been active in a Christian church to work with a shaman or medicine man while also receiving pastoral care from a minister. Sweat lodges, vision quests, prayer circles, and other rituals may be utilized from tribal traditions to facilitate healing. My experience with Native American spirituality has taught me to honor a broader spectrum of practices and has expanded my interpretation of spiritual healing. Pastors should be open-minded and educated about spiritual disciplines beyond their particular tradition.

Earth-centered spirituality, Wiccan religion, druidism, and Celtic spirituality have all seen a resurgence of interest. If a pastor is unfamiliar with a person's spiritual resources, listen to the meaning, purpose, and value it gives and incorporate these spiritual strengths into your pastoral care plan. On the other hand, if cult and ritual abuse has been present or suspected, the person may need to find new and entirely different practices to nurture his or her spiritual growth.

SUICIDE AND CRISIS INTERVENTION

The stress of trauma can become so intense as to seem overwhelming. Depression and its related somatic disturbances is common. Some victims of violence feel responsibility for what happened, which may lead to feelings of guilt, sinfulness, worthlessness, and the conclusion that life is not worth living. It is not inevitable that depression will lead to suicidal thoughts. There is no single cause of suicide. However, it is important for all pastors to be aware of the signs of suicide, especially when working with the PTSD population.

Any prior history of a suicide attempt is a strong indicator that suicide may be threatened again. "Twelve percent of persons who attempt suicide will try again and succeed within two years" (Grollman, 1988, p. 64). Many people who plan to take their life will speak about it ahead of time, both in direct and subtle ways. Pastors should be attuned to comments such as, "After she's gone, I'm going to kill myself."

I had a parishioner, Barbara (not her real name), who was a survivor of multiple incidents of sexual abuse by her father during her childhood. As an adult, after undergoing therapy for a couple of years, she arrived in my office seeking spiritual counseling in a desire to feel better about herself as a person. She needed to believe that God did not see her as "dirty" or "blame" her for what she "had allowed to happen." She had many questions about "how God could let this happen" to her. This woman's mother was a devout Christian who told her daughter, "I am praying for your healing and that some day you will forgive your father."

While I was working with Barbara, her mother became terminally ill with metastatic cancer. One day, Barbara called to ask if we could have an unscheduled meeting. She said, "I got some upsetting news and I need to talk to you." In my office, she revealed that her mother had only a couple of months to live, and in a very direct and nonchalant manner, Barbara announced, "After she dies, I'm going to kill myself. I know how and when I'll do it, and I'm not going to tell anyone in my family."

I had developed a trusting relationship with Barbara and I knew her past mental health history included previous suicide attempts and depression. She was also actively involved with a local therapist, whom we had met with together on two occasions. I knew I must not only take Barbara's threat seriously, I had to remain calm and intervene.

My first step was to take Barbara's threat seriously and my reflective listening would let her know my attitude of acceptance of her was unshaken. I acknowledged that it had taken great courage on her part to share her feelings and that I appreciated her honesty. I also knew she had gotten through similar feelings in the past, so after she described some specifics about how she would kill herself, I asked, "What stopped you in the past from taking action?" Barbara said that she had been in contact with her therapist who had helped her through past experiences, but this time "no one will be able to stop me, because no one will know when I'm going to do it." Then I asked her if she would brainstorm with me some alternatives that she had not thought about. This led us into a discussion of what she had been feeling upon the news of her mother's declining health. During this time, she revealed her anger at her mother for not stopping her father from abusing her as a child, and for eventually forgiving him and remarrying him. Our conversation then focused on what issues she might want to take up with her mother over the next few months and how to approach the subject.

Before Barbara left my office, she also agreed to call her therapist and make an appointment to see her as soon as possible. I made certain that I did not try to offer her hope through false reassurances, but I believe as pastoral counselors we do represent and can offer hope by our faith in God's presence in the struggle. I let Barbara know that I believed a solution could be found to allay her desperation and we scheduled another appointment to meet later in the week. We also made a "contract" that if she felt like hurting herself, she would call her therapist and/or me. Later that same day, with Barbara's permission, I called her therapist. We discussed the role each of us would take in supporting Barbara through her mother's illness and death.

Over the next four months, Barbara and I met regularly and took long walks together, talking about her relationship with her mom—the good things as well as the disappointments. She also imagined what kind of a relationship she desired to have with her mom, and what could be accomplished reasonably in the time they had left together. We ended our meetings with a brief prayer asking for God's presence, guidance, and support through these difficult times.

This case has a happy ending. Barbara's mother died in a hospital bed with her children and her husband at her side. I was also there and prayed with her family. A funeral was held a few days later. Barbara's mother had been open to hearing all she had to say about the past and the present and reconciliation was reached. Barbara has also been able to reach out to her aging father.

Sometimes, intervention is not successful and a suicide occurs. When comforting the bereaved family of the suicide, basic grief counseling methods are employed, but the pastor must keep in mind the social stigma attached to death by suicide. Most communities have special grief recovery programs for families of suicide victims, and pastors should be aware of these for referrals. At the funeral for a person who has committed suicide, the pastor should refrain from any hint at blasphemy. The eulogy should celebrate the positive aspects of the person's life and the ways in which his or her life was a blessing.

In the spectrum of crises that pastors encounter, suicide is only one. A parishioner who had been in therapy for a year came to my office hysterical because her husband told her he wanted a divorce. He could not deal with her emotional problems any longer. She had been processing flashbacks from sexual assault, and had begun to deal with years of sexual identity issues. Crisis ministry is part of all pastoral care settings. Crisis intervention is a method of assisting individuals to cope with critical moments in their lives.

A pastor's response and support may enable a person to come through a crisis with a greater level of spiritual health. All crises are spiritual at the core because they involve issues that will call for reflection on one's values, purpose, and meaning in life. I believe one of the most important things a pastor has to offer is a relationship that communicates that life has significance, beauty, and hope.

The "ABC" method of crisis intervention recommended by Howard W. Stone, professor of pastoral care and pastoral psychology and author of the book *Crisis Counseling* (1976), begins with Achieving a relationship of trust and compassion grounded in good listening skills. Next, the problem must be Boiled down to its basic issues by helping the person to focus on relevant components. The final stage is Coping by taking action. Discussions with the person in crisis will explore goals that are achievable; resources available to meet those goals; alternative kinds of actions that might achieve the goals; taking action; and review of the action for possible revision. At all times, the pastor should be working a process of intervention only to the extent that he or she is competent to perform. Without training in psychology or certification in pastoral counseling, the pastor should be working with a qualified therapist and be in communication with a personal supervisor on a regular basis for support and guidance.

Chapter 8

Healing Rituals

Mutuality is movement; bringing one another to life.

Carter Heyward (1993)

Those who are healing from trauma and the resulting side effects, such as PTSD, may benefit from the use of some demonstrative and symbolic means of acknowledging the harm and celebrating the process of recovery. The religious background and spirituality of the individual will help determine what kind of ritual will be useful. Sometimes this is carried out in a group setting; for others it is done privately or with the pastor. There are limitless possibilities that the pastor can explore with the person and it is essential that he or she be included in the actual creation of the ritual to the degree desired. Several books listed in the bibliography are excellent resources for examples of healing rituals. The ones that I use most frequently are *Human Rites: Worship Resources for an Age of Change,* compiled by Hanna Ward and Jennifer Wild (1995); *She Who Dwells Within: A Feminist Vision of Renewed Judaism,* by Lynn Gottlieb (1995); and, from the Wiccan tradition, *Truth or Dare,* by Starhawk (1987).

During my early years as an Anglican priest, several women who were survivors of sexual and domestic violence spoke to me about how difficult it was for them to participate in the traditional Sunday service of worship and communion, yet they longed for reconnection to their Christian tradition. Together, a small group of us reflected on the themes and symbols that we found healing; we then created a liturgy of communion and healing that was sensitive to the use of language and symbols. I am including that service in its evolving format here for your use. Consider it as a guide for creating a liturgy that meets the needs of the person(s) you are working with. It has undergone several revisions and I regret that I am not able to recall the original resources that inspired some of the wording.

The original goal in the creation of the liturgy was to provide a ritual of communion in the Christian tradition that avoided use of language that triggered flashbacks in survivors of abuse. Particularly troublesome were the traditional words of consecration, "Take, eat. This is my body, given (broken) for you." Survivors of incest who were subjected to forced oral sex had a great deal of difficulty hearing these words. For survivors of ritual abuse, the consecration of the wine, "Drink of this all of you; for this is my blood of the new covenant which is poured out for many for the forgiveness of sins," was too reminiscent of animal sacrifice and the forced drinking of blood. One young woman had been subjected to both ritual abuse and incest by her father, an ordained minister, who intentionally used the communion liturgy as part of the ritual abuse setting. Eventually, after intensive therapy, she was able to participate in the liturgy of communion and healing.

It is also important to be sensitive to references of God as "Father" and the use of the male pronoun. Discuss this with the people you are working with. For some, it is healing to use the masculine language and reclaim God as a benevolent male figure in their lives. For others, it is too uncomfortable and all masculine language must be eliminated, replaced by feminine or gender-neutral references.

The use of candles in religious ceremonies is common, but candles are also heavily used in many cults and abusive rituals. Other symbols of hope and new life can be used, such as fruit, flowers, eggs, water, etc. Give careful thought to your surroundings and the creation of the altar. It may not be possible to hold the service in the church sanctuary initially. Another quiet space can be prepared appropriately. If the sanctuary is being used, remember to recreate the space as necessary to honor the needs of the people involved.

The first public celebration of a similar version of the liturgy of communion and healing took place in St. John's Anglican Church in Kitchener, Ontario, Canada, on the one-year anniversary of the Montreal Massacre. Over 200 women and men, many of whom I knew as survivors of trauma, came into the church sanctuary to receive communion for the first time in years and to acknowledge the tragedy of violence against women. The liturgy that evening was framed by readings and music filled with hope and themes of resurrection. The distribution of communion was preceded by a dance that brought the people into position encircling the altar and the sanctuary. We all joined hands for the postcommunion prayer and benediction. It was one of the most powerful, spirit-filled experiences of my life. When a pastor allows the flexibility of deviating from the tradition in the process of discerning a healing liturgy, God is revealed in new and dynamic ways.

A LITURGY OF COMMUNION AND HEALING

Gathering to Worship

LEADER: We give thanks, God of wonder, for the marvel of creation that surrounds us,

ALL: and for all the wonders of life you make known to us.

LEADER: Let us see your glory, your justice, and your peace.

ALL: May our lives and our world be reawakened and healed by the power of your grace.

LEADER and ALL OTHERS: Amazing God, to you all hearts are open, all desires known, and from you no secrets are hidden. Guide our hearts by the inspiration of your Holy Spirit, that we may completely love you, and honestly magnify your holy name; through Christ our Redeemer. Amen.

Invocation

LEADER: We give you thanks, Gentle One who has touched our soul. You have loved us from even before the moment of our first waking and have held us in joy and in grief.

ALL: Stay with us, we pray. Grace us with your presence, and with it, the fullness of our own humanity. Help us claim our strength and need, our awesomeness and fragile beauty, that encouraged by the truth, we might work to restore compassion to the human family and renew the face of the earth. Amen.

Proclamation of the Word

Suggested readings: Isaiah 42:1-4 (NRSV); Ps. 91 from Rienstra, 1992, *Swallow's Nest,* p. 197; Luke 13:10-13 (NRSV); "Giving It to the Wind" from Bass and Davis, 1988, *The Courage to Heal,* p. 399. (Silence may follow the readings.)

Intercessions/Prayers of the People

LEADER: Divine One, transform us with your compassion. In the power of your radiant love we place our concerns.

For those at risk: the victims of violence, abuse, poverty, injustice, and greed.

ALL: Protect them from harm, empower them to survive, and liberate them to thrive in authentic life.

LEADER: For those who are sick: those struggling with mental illness, addictions and compulsive behavior, the pain and suffering of HIV, AIDS, hepatitis, cancer, and other debilitating illnesses.

ALL: Give them strength, courage, and openness to receive healing in its many forms.

LEADER: For those dealing with traumatic pasts: those who are recovering memories of childhood sexual abuse, those who have been raped or ritually abused, and all other violations of body, mind, and spirit.

ALL: Make your comfort and compassion known to them, and send them friends and counselors to affirm them as sacred beings made in your image. Renew them so that they may have abundant life.

LEADER: For those who have been perpetrators of abuse.

ALL: Open their hearts and minds to see the deep hurt they cause. Help them acknowledge their wrongs, take full responsibility for the abuse, and lead them to repentance so they may walk a new path.

LEADER: For those who are entrusted power, influence, and authority: teachers, clergy, executives, politicians, parents, law enforcement officials, doctors, and therapists.

ALL: Keep them mindful of their privilege, and guide them to a just, fair, and respectful partnership, always working to create mutuality in their relationships.

LEADER: For those who are dying: especially those who are alone.

ALL: Let your loving presence be known to them, and grant them a peaceful entry into the Light.

LEADER: For all creation: the moons, stars, and galaxies that are the universe. The water, air, animals, and plants that make the earth a livable place for humankind.

ALL: Teach us to care for, respect, and protect our world. Make all who share earth's fragile beauty active contributors to its healing and stewards of its sacredness.

LEADER: Healing Spirit—

ALL: —receive our prayers.

Confession

ALL: Merciful God, we confess that we have failed to love ourselves. We remember that we have looked on our bodies with dislike and distrust. We have denied our own feelings, and have been separated from our self, God, and others. We remember the trap of secrecy that kept us from sharing our fear and pain. We remember that we believed we were responsible for the violence that happened to us. We have not trusted in our own strength and potential.

LEADER: You are invited to share your own confessions silently or aloud. Let us share our confession of needs.

ALL: We need to be healed of pain and sorrow. We need to break the silence and touch the world with our truth. We need to trust and appreciate our bodies. We need to affirm our feelings, believe in our anger, trust in our loving kindness. We need to release our hearts from bondage. We want to live free knowing that beyond the brokenness there can be wholeness.

Words of Pardon and Grace

LEADER: In Jesus Christ, God knows and receives us as we are. Listen, give thanks, and live.

The Passing of the Peace

LEADER: The peace of Christ be always with you.

ALL: And also with you. [Greet one another with the peace of Christ as you feel comfortable in doing.]

Offertory Sentence

LEADER: Let us give thanks to El Shaddai for She alone is good!

Prayer Over the Gifts

LEADER: God of love and mercy, your word stirs within us the expectation of the arrival of your Son. Accept all we offer you and sustain us with your promise of eternal life. We ask this in the name of Jesus Christ our Brother.

Eucharistic Prayer

CELEBRANT: God be with you.

PEOPLE: And also with you.

CELEBRANT: Open your hearts.

PEOPLE: We open them to God.

CELEBRANT: Let us give thanks to our God.

PEOPLE: It is right to give God thanks and praise.

CELEBRANT: O God, sustainer of the universe, you are worthy of glory and praise.

PEOPLE: Glory to you for ever and ever.

CELEBRANT: It is good and joyful that in your presence we give thanks, Holy God, for you have included us in creation and made us in your glorious image. You have remembered us from our beginning and fed us with your constant love; you have redeemed us in Jesus Christ and knit us into one community. Through your Spirit you replenish us and call us to fullness of life.

Therefore, with the woman who gave you birth, the women and men who befriended you, who argued with you and reached out to you, the woman who anointed you for death, the friends who met you, risen from the dead, and with all who have loved you throughout the ages, we praise you saying:

ALL: Holy, holy, holy, vulnerable God, heaven and earth are full of your glory; hosanna in the highest. Blessed is the one who comes in the name of God; hosanna in the highest.

CELEBRANT: Most generous, self-giving God, we celebrate your gift of creation. We rejoice that you have formed us in your image and called us to dwell in your infinite love.

You gave the world into our care that we might be your faithful stewards and reflect your bountiful grace. Through Abraham and Sarah you blessed us with a holy heritage. You delivered us from slavery, sustained us in the wilderness, and raised up prophets that we might realize the fullness of your promise.

But we failed to recognize your image in ourselves; we were numb and could not experience your goodness in the world around us and so we rejected your love.

United with us by incarnation through Mary and the Holy Spirit and born into the human family, Jesus showed us the way of freedom and life. Walking among us, he touched us with healing and transforming power, and showed us your glory.

ALL: Holy One who gathers us, we need to feel more deeply the bonds that are truly nurturing, sustaining, and healing. We remember that long ago, Jesus gathered together his friends, took bread, said the blessing, broke the bread. Giving it to his friends, he said, "Take this bread. For this is my life which is given for you. Do this in remembrance of me."

CELEBRANT: In the same way after supper he took the cup of wine, blessed it, and said, "Drink this, all of you. This is my love, poured out for all. Whenever you drink, do this for the remembrance of me."

ALL: We remember his death on the cross, we proclaim the resurrection to new life, we await the return of Christ in glory.

CELEBRANT: We pray that even as Jesus was able to go forward from that night with the strength and support he gained from you, his God, and from his friends, we might be able to do the same.

Pour out your love and your blessing on all we offer here. Breathe your Spirit into these gifts of bread and wine, to make of them the Life and Love of Christ. Let your Spirit who broods over the whole creation dwell with us.

Jesus' Prayer to God

CELEBRANT: Let us pray.

ALL: Eternal Spirit, Life-Giver, Pain-Bearer, Justice-Maker, Source of all that is and that shall be, the One who loves us all, Compassionate God in whom is heaven: the hallowing of your name echoes throughout the universe. The Way of Justice be followed by the people of the world. Your heavenly will be done by all created beings. Your commonwealth of peace and freedom sustain our hope and come on earth. With the bread that we need for today, feed us. In the hurts we absorb from one another, forgive us. In times of temptation and test, strengthen us. From trials too great to endure, spare us. From the grip of all that is evil, free us. For you live in the glory of the power that is love, now and forever. Amen.

Breaking of the Bread

CELEBRANT: We are one Bread, one Life.

ALL: We will love one another as Christ loves us.

CELEBRANT: The gifts of God for the people of God. Take them in remembrance of Christ and seek him in your heart, and be empowered by faith, with thanksgiving.

Words of Distribution

> The Life of Christ, the Bread of Justice.
> The Love of Christ, the Wine of Liberation.

Postcommunion Prayer

ALL: Holy, gracious, and loving God, you have drawn us to your heart and nourished us at your table with holy food and drink. Now send us forth to be your people in the world and to proclaim your truth, this day and ever more. Amen.

Blessing and Dismissal

ALL: May God the Righteous Judge, Loving Protector, and Tender Healer bless us and all people this day with justice, protection, and healing, according to our needs. Amen.

(Suggest closing the gathering with the singing of "Song of the Soul" by Cris Williamson. Music/hymns should be inserted into the liturgy as needed.)

Chapter 9

Good News in Scripture

To believe in the resurrection means that we cannot stop at our wounds.

Patricia McCarthy

In their journey of healing from PTSD, some people will be confronting theological issues, particularly those mentioned in Chapter 5. For some of these people, the Bible may be a source of help and inspiration. For others, the Bible may have been used as a means of exacerbating their guilt or as a way of influencing them to stay in abusive relationships, especially women in situations of domestic violence. Although Scripture was intended to be a means of liberation for Jews and Christians, some people who feel alienated from church and God have rejected all Scripture. But for those who seek reconciliation and spiritual healing with their religious heritage, it is imperative that pastors, chaplains, and pastoral caregivers/counselors be aware of how Scripture has been used to oppress, and also know which Scriptures offer messages of salvation and healing.

Clergy who are ill-prepared to deal with persons with PTSD and who lack a basic understanding of traumatic stress may unintentionally quote Scripture or preach a religious viewpoint that exacerbates the PTSD by creating or intensifying shame, guilt, or anxiety. However, pastoral care that reinforces such spiritual values as hope, forgiveness, reconciliation, love, compassion, and justice are likely to contribute to a person's ability to regain peace and wholeness.

Should a pastor sense that Scripture would be a useful resource, the following should be kept in mind. Several metaphors and images in the Hebrew Scripture symbolize God in relationship to his rebellious people, similar to a husband punishing his wife. The prophet Hosea, for example, symbolizes God in many violent exchanges with

Israel, his wife. Hosea's writings can be seen as reflecting a typical pattern of the cycle of battering.

The writings of the prophet Isaiah have many comforting images of deliverance and redemption, such as Isaiah 25:4a; 40:11; 42:1-9; 3:1-4a; 49:8-16; 51:21-23; 61:1-3; 65:1-3a,8; 66:13-1a. However, other passages have been used to show how God punishes women who flaunt their bodies, thereby "asking for it": Isaiah 3:16-17. Pastors should be patient with women who do not find solace in the Hebrew Scriptures, especially in view of the biblical violence against women found in Dinah's rape in Genesis 34, Tamar's rape in 2 Samuel 13:1-22, the sacrifice of Jepthah's daughter in Judges 11, and the murder and mutilation of the unnamed concubine from Bethlehem in Judges 19:1-30. Women who have read the Bible and are familiar with passages such as these may feel they are somehow part of an ongoing pattern in Christian history which shows that God does not intervene for women's sakes.

There are many positive images and stories available in the Hebrew Scripture that can be recommended. Ezekiel 37:1-14, known as the "Valley of Dry Bones," can be a particularly inspiring passage to someone deep in despair as it speaks of God breathing new life into a restored body.

The Book of Job is frequently referenced in terms of a righteous person's suffering. Although Job's anger, anguish, and despair may resonate with a suffering person, the pastor should beware of the statement it carries concerning God's role in "testing" a person's faith by inflicting suffering. This is not a redeeming perspective for most victims.

Many of the Psalms reflect the questions of suffering people throughout the ages. Psalm 5 asks God to listen to a cry for help and trusts that God will punish evildoers. Psalm 9:9 describes God as a "refuge for the oppressed; a stronghold in times of trouble" (New International Version). Psalm 11 affirms God's love of justice. The author of Psalm 13:2 refers to "wrestling with my thoughts" and "sorrow in my heart" (NIV), common feelings in those with PTSD. The message that God will not abandon the faithful and will show the "path of life" (NIV) is expressed in Psalm 16:11. The author of Psalm 22, quoted by Jesus from the Cross, speaks of a suffering person who feels abandoned by God, but who believes God cannot be too far off. Psalm 28 asks God for protection and mercy. As is true with most of the Psalms, Psalm 30 is an image of a God who controls all of one's life. It also praises God as a healer who "brought me up from the grave" (NIV Psalm 30:3). A beautifully lyrical search for God in the midst of a downcast soul and suffering "mortal agony" (NIV) is found in Psalm 42:10.

For someone who has been a perpetrator of violence or other behavior that makes them heavy with guilt feelings, Psalm 51 is a prayer for healing and moral renewal. For victims of violence by someone familiar or close to them, Psalm 55 acknowledges the pain of betrayal and God's disdain of breach of trust.

Psalm 77 is a prayer for deliverance from personal trouble and speaks of the author's mental agony that leads to a questioning of God's justice and love, but recalls God's intervention on behalf of the Israelites during the Exodus—escape from Pharaoh. The psalmist who wrote 86:7 prays for God's help and laments the "day of trouble" (NIV), but expresses confidence in God's steadfast love and faithfulness.

Verse 10 in Psalm 103 declares that God does not bring suffering upon people, even those who have sinned: "He does not deal with us according to our sins, nor repay us according to our iniquities" (NRSV).

Other Hebrew Scriptures that stand out include Deuteronomy 30: 19-20 which speaks to the benefit of choosing life over death when faced with despair.

When working with someone who is abusing their partner, Malachi 2:13-16 upholds the sacredness of the marital covenant, at least in terms of faithfulness and loyalty, as God is faithful and loyal to us. Unfortunately, the passage also emphasizes the sole purpose of marriage to be offspring, and it says God "hates divorce" (NRSV). But it also says God hates "covering one's garment with violence" (NRSV). Discernment is especially necessary for pastoral use of this passage.

Veterans who have been involved in killing, may carry tremendous guilt. If they are seeking God's forgiveness, or if they believe God can never forgive them for the atrocities they committed, these passages may be helpful: Isaiah 44:22, "I have swept away your offenses like a cloud, your sins like the morning mist. Return to me, for I have redeemed you" (NIV); Isaiah 43:25, "I, even I, am he who blots out your transgressions, for my own sake" (NIV); Micah 7:19, "He will again have compassion upon us; he will tread our iniquities under foot. You will hurl all our sins into the depths of the sea" (NIV). Coming to believe that no sin is greater than God's capacity to forgive is a major step toward feeling restored.

The Christian Scripture has some troublesome passages that stand out. Matthew 6:33-34 has a message about not worrying and living in the moment while seeking God's righteousness, which can be comforting to a person dealing with anxiety reduction, but it is dangerous advice to a woman in a violent domestic setting who needs to take immediate action to secure her safety.

Luke 6:27-36 is the well-known "love your enemies . . . turn the other cheek" passage that is also potentially destructive advice to an abused person. This Scripture was never intended to validate abusive or violent behavior or to encourage a Christian to seek victimization. Such ideas are contrary to Jesus' message of love of oneself.

Luke 17:3-4 concerns how often we are to forgive someone who "sins against you" (NRSV). When used out of context, it can be interpreted as advisable to forgive a perpetrator of violence, even "seven times a day," and to allow that person continued access to their victim. This view totally ignores the seriousness of the meaning of repentance, and Jesus' expectation that a "sinner" must repent in order to qualify for forgiveness.

The Gospel of Luke also has helpful scripture. Luke 13:10-16 is the story of the healing of the bent-over woman on the Sabbath. Her restoration to fullness from whatever was "crippling" her is an example of Jesus' power to bring about recover from chronic, life-altering illness. By his actions, Jesus also shows that a woman's need for healing takes precedent over religious laws prohibiting healing on the Sabbath, thereby demonstrating his high value of women in a patriarchal culture.

Luke 15:11-32, the parable of the prodigal son, represents God's abundant mercy and forgiveness toward a person who lived for a while with a lifestyle that could be judged contemptible. This passage has been helpful to some veterans who committed wartime atrocities and others who perpetrated trauma. The story reveals God's steadfast love.

The parable of the persistent widow in Luke 18:1-8 may inspire hope, tenacity, and the ability not to give up when a trauma victim is seeking justice in the court system. In the story, her persistence wins out over the judge's repeated disinterest in her pleas for "justice against my adversary" (NIV).

Jesus' healing of a woman who had been bleeding for 112 years in Luke 8:3-48 is significant from a historical, cultural, and religious perspective. Women in first-century Palestine who were bleeding or menstruating were considered to be ritually unclean by Jewish purity codes and therefore untouchable lest the person they came in contact with became unclean. Jesus is not offended, nor does he express fear of uncleanliness when the bleeding woman touches his cloak. Instead, she receives immediate healing in a public forum. This story may be helpful to a person who has been raped and who feels "dirty," outcast, or unclean in some way. Jesus demonstrates overcoming the boundary of the religious taboo and shows his desire for her to be socially accepted again.

Women or men who have been reluctant to ask for the help they need may be empowered by Matthew 7:7-11. Luke 4:18-19 is Jesus speaking Isaiah's words of salvation from God. If someone is doubting they are deserving of God's grace, John 10:10 is Jesus' promise of abundant life.

One of the most powerful and encompassing messages of God's expansive mercy was written by Paul to the people in Rome. "For I am convinced that neither death, nor life, nor angels, nor rulers, nor things present, nor things to come, nor powers, nor height, nor depth, nor anything else in all creation will be able to separate us from the love of God in Christ Jesus our Lord" (Romans 8:38-39 NRSV).

Images of God the Father abound in scripture, hymns, prayers, and other resources used in Christian worship. Exclusive reference to the Father God not only leaves out more inclusive descriptions of God, it may be creating a barrier to spiritual healing for certain people, especially women and men who have been violated by men. Pastors should use a variety of metaphors for God, and when providing pastoral care to victims of male-perpetrated violence, be prepared to offer names and metaphors for God that meet the victim's spiritual needs. Some suggestions include: in Hebrew, "El Shaddai," usually translated in the Bible as "God of high places," but equally accurate "God of two breasts"; Exodus 19:4, God as mother eagle; Isaiah 21:3, God as a woman in labor; Isaiah 49:15, God as a mother who never forgets her children; Hosea 13:8, God as a mother bear caring for her cubs; (Apocrypha) Sirach 1:14ff., God as female/Wisdom cocreator present with male God from the beginning; Matthew 23:37, Jesus/God as a hen gathering her chicks; Luke 15:8-10, God as a woman searching for what is lost.

Non–gender-specific biblical names for God include: Wonderful Counselor, Rock, Holy One, Emmanuel, Prince of Peace, Creator; and Jesus: Light of the World, the Word Made Flesh, Bread, Water, Redeemer, Servant, Savior.

When praying with victims of PTSD, pastors can open the way to new images by using such inclusive images of God as Sacred Breath, Healing Spirit Within, Spirit of Life, Source of Infinite Love, Wounded Healer, the Still Presence, Source of All Life, Seeker of the Lost, Nurturing God, Peaceful Harbor. Free yourself up to image and describe God in ways that reflect how the victim is feeling: Silent God, Distant Power, Puzzling God, Angry God, Forgiving God, Gentle One, Mighty One, Ruler of the Universe, Hidden God, Giver of Hope, Compassionate One, God of Justice, Lord of Tears, Great Mystery, Lord of Tender Patience, Amazing Grace, God of My Struggle, Befriender of the Lonely, God of Dreams. The possibilities are infinite with the guidance of the Holy Spirit.

Discovering alternative images of God can be a liberating experience for those persons whose religious experience has confined them solely to traditional representations of the deity. By validating their search for spiritual healing and renewal with a diverse expression of who or what God may be, a pastor can inspire hope for new meaning and reconnection to something that has been meaningful to them in the past. The path to complete restoration includes spiritual healing and encompasses growth and development at many levels.

Usually, emotional healing is a lengthy process after a significant traumatic event. One of the reasons holistic healing is sought is to allow for more than release from the acute pain. When spiritual healing is also addressed, the power of the Creator moves the person beyond the event and offers guidance into greater maturity and understanding. Eventually, victims' emotional and psychological wounds are healed and their character grows as well. Character development, which is enhanced by gaining spiritual insight and healing, is essential for a survivor of trauma to rebound effectively from future hurts and losses that inevitably will occur.

Chapter 10

Working with Therapists, Counselors, and Doctors

God is never closer than when the space between two hearts narrows.

Joan Borysenko

At some point after a traumatic event, a victim will most likely seek treatment from a psychiatrist, psychologist, psychotherapist, medical doctor, clinical mental health counselor, social worker, or any combination of the above. It is possible that the victim has one or more of these connections in place before contacting a pastor, chaplain, or pastoral counselor. Or it may be that the victim comes to the clergy or pastoral counselor first, who will then help find a referral to the appropriate support and treatment in the mental health arena.

However the sequence unfolds, pastors caring for persons with PTSD can be most effective when they are working together on the victim's behalf as an integral part of the health care team, creating a full biopsychosocial-spiritual approach to treating PTSD. For pastors to be successful in making referrals and sustaining relationships with these other professionals, there are recommended procedures and guidelines to follow, beginning with how pastors handle their own pastoral counseling.

Every pastor should be familiar with their denominational requirements and restrictions regarding the duration of counseling time allowed on a particular issue with a person, and any professional certifications that may be required to perform counseling in the church community. Because of the number of cases of reported sexual abuse by clergy, most denominations now place restrictions, or at least have recommendations and guidelines, limiting clergy to crisis intervention and brief counseling. It is also highly recommended that all active clergy members have a supervisor, mentor, or professional counselor that they see on a regular basis to debrief their reactions, transferences, countertransference, projections, or other concerns that will arise when counseling and providing pastoral care. Not only does this provide added safety for victims seeking counseling, it is a proactive form of clergy self-care (see Chapter 11).

Most clergy receive minimal education in the area of clinical mental health while in seminary. Learning the language of medical and psychiatric practitioners will help the pastor when offering support and referrals. A pastor should gain at least enough knowledge and awareness to recognize those persons who need psychiatric or medical care. Any pastor who has been out of seminary for ten years or more and has not participated in ongoing continuing education should consider courses in human sexuality, drug and alcohol and related addictions, domestic and sexual violence, PTSD, basic mental disorders, and human growth and development. Local colleges and professional mental health organizations have continuing education courses and conferences that will help pastors stay current. Your local hospital may have a library with mental health resources and a continuing education division that can let you know what is being offered in your region. Tell the mental health professionals with whom you network that you would like to be aware of seminars that will enhance your pastoral ministry and offer them information you have about spirituality and health education.

One of the first steps in providing spiritual counseling for someone with PTSD is listening well. A pastor should be gathering information that will help reveal what the traumatized person understands about his or her problem, the kind of help he or she is seeking, and the issues the pastor will be able to address. It is advisable for you, the pastor, to consider taking notes to reflect the goals of your work and how you plan to carry them out. These notes should be considered confidential and kept in a locked file. However, if your denomination has as a strict understanding of privileged communication because of the Rite of Confession, notes may not be appropriate at times. It is best to seek advice from denominational leadership.

To help the pastor assess a trauma survivor's needs when it is not a crisis situation (Chapter 7), it is useful to have a checklist to help conduct a spiritual assessment and evaluate the current status of the survivor's support system. If the person is not well known to you, having a history of his or her religious involvement will be helpful. Note if he or she is, or has been, involved with recovery groups such as AA, chronic illness support groups, grief counseling, parenting education, marriage enrichment, conflict mediation, divorce counseling, mental health counseling, social worker counseling, mentoring, spiritual direction, alternative healing, hobbies, and other interests. Record the names and phone numbers of vital people in his or her life.

As part of your caregiver/pastor's record, you may want to document the reason that you were approached for pastoral care by stating the presenting problem, and the goals that were established for addressing it. If you refer the person to another resource, make note of who it is and the reason for the referral.

In preparation for making referrals, it is advisable that pastors become familiar with the individuals, organizations, and agencies in their community that represent the professional and spiritual values of the person you are referring for care. Keep a list of medical doctors, mental health professionals, including family counselors, addictions counselors, social workers, wellness practitioners, lawyers, spiritual directors, and hospital chaplains, whom you have met or spoken with about their qualifications and philosophy.

A list of crisis hotline phone numbers should be readily available to you at all times, such as rape and domestic violence centers, child abuse prevention (Parents Anonymous), and suicide prevention (Samaritans). Some community mental health counseling centers have twenty-four-hour telephone assistance.

You will also want to have the local phone numbers of twelve-step groups, grief groups, chronic illness support, living with cancer groups, AIDS groups, gay/lesbian/bisexual/transgendered groups, PFLAG—Parents and Friends of Lesbians and Gays, and caregiver support groups.

Knowing where to secure shelter for homeless people and battered women and their children is essential. Treatment and rehabilitation centers for those suffering addictions are also worth knowing about, and taking a visit to view the conditions and environment is a good idea.

The need for a medical evaluation may arise very soon after the onset of a traumatic event. For victims of domestic and sexual violence, having to expose their bodies to a stranger for medical examination may be extremely difficult and may feel like a continuation of the violation. Issues of shame and humiliation may be exacerbated. Volunteers at rape and domestic violence crisis centers are trained to accompany victims to initial medical visits. The presence of a pastor or chaplain who has an established relationship with the victim may be helpful, but should not be forced on the person. The pastor should always ask the person if he or she wants the pastor present; there should be no assumption that this is the case. Support, reassurance, and listening will go a long way in helping the victim through the acute crisis phase.

If, at any point, the victim requests your presence during a medical visit, it is possible you will be expected to help the victim remember everything the doctor has said. To assist with the recollection of the information from the doctor, pastors should have some familiarity with basic medical terminology and be assertive in empowering the victim to ask questions of the doctor should anything be unclear. Keep in mind that as a third party in the room, the doctor may begin to address attention to you rather than the victim through direct eye contact and by offering paperwork, etc., to you. This is an opportunity to remind the doctor to speak to the victim and allow the person to begin to reclaim personal power should he or she feel up to it emotionally.

When making a referral, especially for a person with PTSD for whom trust may be a major issue, the referral becomes an extension of the relationship you have established with the trauma survivor. The survivor is going to expect that you trust and believe in the person you are recommending. It will be easier to send the survivor with confidence to a person or agency if you have laid the groundwork for a working relationship ahead of time. It is possible that there will be occasions when you are included in some aspect of the survivor's treatment with the mental health worker or social worker who has taken on his or her long-term treatment. More and more therapists are beginning to see the advantage of working as a team, and the value to incorporating the client's spiritual needs in the overall treatment plan. Staying in communication with each other is critical to an effective relationship and to reinforce the empowerment of the client in terms of their active involvement in the care plan and its implementation. The flow of information and care among all the professionals involved and the client creates a model of healing that is integrated and grounded in a sense of community.

When counseling and treatment leads to growth and healing, those of us in the pastoral care field will give the credit to the creative, life-giving Spirit of God. The transformative energy of Spirit entering into a counseling relationship, in which the wounded person is open in his or her mind and body, may lead to healing in spite of what the pastor has said or done. Keeping in mind that pastors are meant to be channels for the Spirit's healing power will act as a reminder that at best pastors have finite abilities and are more likely to be of help when grounded in their own spiritual relationship with the source of healing. Pastors and pastoral counselors are cocreators with God and the living Spirit actualizing the divine source of healing within each human soul. The demand of creative ministry requires pastors to feed their own souls and nurture themselves to prevent burnout. Suggestions for clergy self-care are discussed in the next chapter.

Chapter 11

Clergy Self-Care

Come to me, you who are weary and who carry heavy loads, and I will give you rest.

Jesus Christ (Matthew 11:28)

For most pastors, rabbis, and chaplains, providing pastoral care is the largest component of their ministerial duties. Comforting, supporting, counseling, and providing spiritual nurture and guidance to those in crisis, and those with ongoing issues, is both a demanding and rewarding calling. Many pastors, because of their awareness, skills, and training, are sought out by trauma survivors, or they may receive referrals from their colleagues who feel less competent to handle posttrauma cases. Caring pastors, who are ministering in a small community setting, are likely to build close and personal relationships with many of the people who come to them at some point for pastoral care. Intimate relationships make the issue of boundaries and spiritual care for the pastor essential to the prevention of burnout, and to protect the counselee from exploitation.

Working with survivors of trauma is difficult at times. Their stories of injury, their pain, grief, and distress may evoke deep feelings in their caregivers. It is natural for pastors to think about and pray frequently for their traumatized parishioners. Pastors need to be aware of the seriousness of their commitment to enter the intimate space of supporting individuals through their healing journey. As pastors endeavor to support the spiritual, emotional, and psychological recovery process of those who seek their help, it is paramount that pastors stay keenly aware of their own needs, feelings, and limitations.

Maintaining respect for the survivor in the midst of their vulnerability carries a component that allows for pastors to recognize their human limitations by kindly refusing to meet the survivor's need, recognizing that it is not realistic to expect to provide complete support at all times. Gently acknowledging the validity of the person's need accompanied by a simple statement such as, "But I cannot meet it right now," may be the wisest response when the pastor feels overwhelmed, unclear, frustrated or in any way unsure about what is the best thing to do in the moment. This is when the pastor can call upon other members of the network of caregivers that has been established. It is important in communicating the refusal to help that the pastor does not say, or imply, that the need is "wrong" or "bad," or "too much to ask."

Like all people, clergy are subject to burnout at different rates. Depending on their own childhood experiences and how well they have been dealt with pastors may have been conditioned as "rescuers" or "martyrs," always putting the needs of others before their own. Pastor self-neglect may be a signal that their own past history is unresolved, and they could benefit from intentional counseling themselves.

Pastors, similar to other caregivers, are especially at risk for neglecting responsibilities to their spouses/partners and their children. They can be so busy caring for others and so focused on others' needs, that they overlook attending to their own families. Single pastors are at risk for making their ministry their whole life, or the congregation may expect them to be on call at all times. Striking the balance of caregiving to parishioners, counselees, family, and oneself is a challenge. Pastors must be intentional about feeding their own souls and rediscovering their personal sources of spiritual nurturing. Pastors who are spiritually, personally, and intellectually fulfilled are better prepared to minister effectively in their church and community than those who are out of touch with the need for Sabbath and play.

Keeping to the number of hours a pastor is covenanted to work each week will provide a necessary limit that can help prevent overwork. Leaving town on one's days off may be a useful way to experience a sense of a minivacation. Screening calls on the answering machine is another practical way of honoring time off, while still being available for an emergency. However, when pastors are on vacation, they should ask a colleague or qualified lay minister to provide full coverage in their absence.

Under ideal circumstances, pastors will have the supervision of their pastoral counseling paid for by their congregation. At the least, pastors should be participating in a regular clergy support group and have a parish-pastor relations committee that they meet with regularly to discuss the well-being of the pastor in relationship to the expectations of the congregation.

The purpose of pastors becoming intentional about their self-nurture is to seek the strengthening of their spiritual resources in order to protect their mental health, creativity, and primary relationship. Maintaining one's spiritual grounding will assist in reinforcing a pastor's professional identity and encouraging a proactive role in reflecting on pastoral ethics. Defining ethical professional boundaries for those ministering in religious communities has been controversial. Standards of ethical behavior are based on the recognition of the power imbalance that exists between pastor and parishioner. If the pastor's theological interpretation of the pastor/parishioner relationship is one of mutuality, boundaries may be less well defined. The relationship may be flexible and allow for shared authority in some areas and social friendship. A partnership model of ministry helps to dismantle the traditional hierarchical paradigm of church polity. However, the pastor remains the ecclesiastical leader of the congregation in the eyes of the laity. There is implicit power that comes with the position. A pastor has access to parishioners' lives when people are likely to be extremely vulnerable. Should the pastor be particularly needy or fragile spiritually, emotionally, or sexually while attempting to provide pastoral care, there is a high risk for the pastor to excessively self-disclose his or her own problems, creating a level of intimacy that may be misinterpreted or misused. Issues of power, self-disclosure, and intimacy are complicated by gender issues. An excellent source with a more in-depth examination of this topic is *Boundary Wars: Intimacy and Distance in Healing Relationships,* edited by Katherine Hancock Ragsdale (1996).

Boundaries are violated when pastors break confidentiality. In some denominations there are no exceptions to this rule when a disclosure is made during a confession, for example. Other denominations allow breach of confidentiality for protecting the life of the person disclosing or someone they have injured or are threatening to harm. Parishioners may also be hurt when religious professionals use the power of their position for personal gain, such as attempting to have elderly parishioners remember them in their wills with money or material goods of value. When pastors attempt to minister beyond their level of expertise, they are overstepping boundaries based on trust, and they are exploiting the parishioners' vulnerability.

Although there is a need to recognize the necessity for professional boundaries in clergy relationships, it is also important to acknowledge that the very nature of a church community lends itself to close relationships, friendship, and the intimacy of personal disclosure, making boundaries more nebulous in some circumstances. Healing takes place through many of these relationships and sometimes appropriate touch itself can be healing. Nonetheless, discerning boundaries and appropriate behavior in the pastor/parishioner/counselee relationship will be clearest when the pastor is nurtured spiritually. It is essential that pastors remain connected to God in body, mind, and spirit or lest they risk disconnection from themselves. When disconnection sets in, the pastor will not be able to recognize spiritual neglect. Pastors must claim their right and their need to have their spiritual reservoirs filled.

Engaging in self-care on a regular basis contributes to the prevention of burnout and models self-respect. When pastors nurture and replenish themselves, they are better conditioned to create a respectful and comfortable context for pastoral care. Pastors are able to honor and value others and establish appropriate boundaries when they see those who seek their care as distinct individuals worthy of support and respect.

Pastors who thrive in their ministry, and mature spiritually in spite of their own struggles are centered in the Spirit of God. Staying in connection with others who have histories of grace-filled years of ministry, pastors will have companions to share stories and stimulate reflection on their own spiritual journey. Clergy with a passionate ministry who are thriving in their vocations also have hobbies and interests that stimulate their creativity and involvement with the world beyond their pastoral ministry.

An intentional and disciplined plan for clergy spiritual nurture and self-assessment, which I have found personally enlightening, is presented in the program "Bearing Fruit" developed by clergy and laity representatives of the Episcopal Dioceses of Vermont, Western Massachusetts, New Hampshire, and Maine. Major funding for its development was provided by the Cornerstone Project, a ministry of the Episcopal Church Foundation, devoted to providing resources that will contribute to the enhancement of clergy leadership. "Bearing

Fruit" is a process model of reflection on one's ministry and relationships that has been used successfully since its introduction in 1993. The workbook should be used in dialogue with another trusted and respected person or group of people. Each section begins with several thought-provoking questions to stimulate reflection, and to encourage pastors to imagine where their ministry is headed. Areas offered for examination are faith, personal ministry formation, and integration and planning.

When clergy are engaging in conscious ministry, are full of self-awareness, respectfully attend to those who seek their counsel, exhibit professionalism, and show a connection to God, they may be life-sustaining resources, channels of God's healing power to those in need.

Chapter 12

Prevention of PTSD

Every act done in the sunlight of awareness becomes sacred.

Thich Nhat Hanh

Daily rituals and prayers literally keep the world spinning on its axis.

Hopi Native American Saying

Aside from natural disasters, all other sources of traumatic stress are preventable, or at least subject to a reduction in the frequency of occurrence. It could even be argued that natural disasters could be influenced by better stewardship of our global environment and ecology. As clergy with leadership roles in religious communities, how can we effect changes in church and public policy that would contribute to a reduction in the causes of trauma and its aftereffects?

There is a strong theological basis for prevention of trauma in the Judeo-Christian tradition. Followers of Jesus Christ are directed by the Great Commandments, in which Jesus is quoting from Deuteronomy 6:4, to "... 'love the Lord your God with all your heart, and with all your soul, and with all your mind, and with all your strength.' The second is this, 'You shall love your neighbor as yourself.' There is no other commandment greater than these" (Mark 12:28-34). This is grounds for intervention to stop or prevent behavior that is hostile to the love of God or the expression of love of neighbor and self.

The Hebrew Scripture speaks of God's covenant with the people and God's promise of steadfast love and the people's response, which shows reverence to God through the keeping of the Ten Commandments and maintenance of justice. The prophet Micah in 6:8 describes God's need for us to "do justice, and to love kindness, and to walk humbly with your God." One could say that the biblical ethic of love, compassion, and justice mandates action to prevent traumatic events.

One of the frequently heard criticisms about the church and organized religion is that they merely reflect the shortcomings of the surrounding culture and do little to initiate a leading role in overcoming the violence, bias, prejudice, and other life-defeating practices of the conventional world. Particularly in view of the main causes and sources of PTSD, such criticism calls those in leadership roles in the church to reflect seriously on the church's role in prevention of PTSD.

Other than natural disasters, such as floods, tornadoes, hurricanes, avalanches, mudslides, etc., the causes of PTSD outlined in Chapter 1 all have a human source, and all involve abuse of power. The human causes of PTSD reveal a broken connection between the human soul and God. Many of the seemingly "natural" disasters are effected by humanity's impact on the natural environment manifested by global warming, disposal of waste, and careless destruction of ecosystems such as the rain forests. Natural disasters contain an element of the brokenness between humanity and our environment. When God gave woman and man "dominion over every living thing that moves upon the earth" in the story of creation in Genesis 1:26-31 (NRSV), humans were given the responsibility to act as good stewards of God's creation. The way we treat our ecological/natural environment (as well as one another) should be a means of honoring the Creator. Human dominion is meant to reveal God's intention of benevolence and peacefulness. For the church to have a credible role in the prevention of PTSD, it must begin with a critical analysis and revision of some of its historical practices that perpetuate abuse of power, and a hierarchical structure that is paradigmatic of domination rather than partnership.

The Christian church has evolved into an organization that incorporates the power dynamics of patriarchy: a system of social and cultural organization that is hierarchical and male dominated in terms of power and value and in which an extremely small number of people hold the greatest power over the majority. The patriarchal system ranks one's position in power according to class, race, gender, ethnicity, sexuality, religious beliefs, and other norms established by the minority holding power. Access to material goods and capital is dependent upon one's rank in the power structure. When a careful study is made of the kind of power structure Jesus described in his model of a faith community, we find a critique of patriarchy and a proposal for a "kingdom of God" in which the poor and marginalized would be given value and invited into the circle of power to become partners with God in creating a world of equality, mutuality, and inclusiveness. Jesus' ideas concerning the reformation of the existing structures of power brought him into conflict with the religious authorities of his time and the reigning Roman government. Though Christianity has strayed from Jesus' mandate for a dismantling of patriarchy, the contemporary church is still called to repentance and conversion to work toward elimination of the multiple forms of violence that result in PTSD.

Sexual and domestic violence and child abuse are interconnected with patriarchy that is sustained by ideologies and theologies that perpetuate male authority, power, and control over females and children. It is the control-over aspect of patriarchy that makes it susceptible to violence. A more in-depth analysis of the relationship between patriarchy and sexual violence can be found in the essay "Sexual Violence: Patriarchy's Offense and Defense" by Karen L. Bloomquist in *Christianity, Patriarchy, and Abuse: A Feminist Critique* (Brown and Bohn, 1989).

Patriarchy has been given biblical authority through the various writings by Paul that have been interpreted to validate white male supremacy. 1 Corinthians 7:3-4 is a statement about conjugal rights in marriage. Ephesians 5, beginning at verse 21, describes the Christian household. Emphasis has been given to (out of context to verse 22), "Wives be subject to your husbands as you are to the Lord" (NRSV). Continuing on in verse 23, however, Paul tempers this with a call to the principal of mutual subjection where being "the head of the wife" involves responsibility for cherishing and protecting her, not a license for any form of abuse: "Husbands, love your wives . . ." (Ephesians 5:25).

The author of 1 Timothy 2:9-15 states regulations for worship that negates women having any authority over men because of Eve's sin, and addresses the requirement of a woman to remain silent in church "with full submission" to male teaching. The objective in these writings is to maintain order in the church as various worship styles were emerging. The purpose was never to devalue women's roles, but this Scripture has been used in the church to silence women.

It is sound scriptural interpretation to assume that it is Paul's intention in his descriptions of familial and community relationships to honor Jesus' teachings, which would lead to the understanding that Paul seeks a more mutual relationship between husband and wife, male and female, than that which existed in the patriarchal social context of his time. Paul is also making an effort to revise male roles to reflect what Jesus modeled in his encounters with women such as the woman at the well in John 4:5-30, and the woman caught in adultery, John 8:3-11. Although one cannot deny that patriarchy was a reality of the early church described in the Letters of the Christian Scripture, it is also evident in Jesus' teachings in the Gospels that hierarchical power structures would not be part of the realm of God that he sought to establish on earth.

It is crucial for the contemporary Christian church to liberate itself from patriarchy and thereby free both men and women from the destructive power and control it supports, and the violence it legitimates. Conversion from patriarchy can begin in churches by the use of God language and imagery that is not exclusively male. Use of a variety of alternative images that include the feminine aspects of God is a significant step in the dismantling of patriarchy in the church.

The use of power and authority by clergy and other church leaders should be discussed and reviewed to allow for changes that create more mutual sharing of power, and the opportunity for access to power in the church structure by anyone called to serve regardless of faith, gender, race, class, sexual orientation, or handicap. Ecclesiastical power, when exercised as a partnership with rather than dominion over laypeople, is a life-giving paradigm of power.

Abuse of power is always a choice. In the church, pastors have an opportunity to nurture spiritual growth which guides people toward decision making that chooses creative solutions over destructive forces. We may look at violence in our society and wonder where the solution is to be found to end the loss of soul and life. The best source of violence prevention is both political and spiritual. A wellspring of moral conscience dwells inside each person who recognizes the image of God written on his or her heart. The spiritual center of every person holds a vision of transformation that creates a change of heart; a conversion in one's thinking that seeks the best of our religious traditions and the best that lies within us. Our human potential for sin is weakened by the strengthening of our invisible ties to the divine.

Therein lies our hope, and hope is a powerful force for change. Hope involves new perspectives and possibilities when all seems lost. Hope is an antidote for despair. It is the faith that life will rise out of death.

Nevertheless, realistically, human conflict will never end. Therefore, we must reexamine how we handle conflict, locally and globally. The church has a major role to play in learning, utilizing, and teaching conflict resolution through negotiation and mediation. Most faith communities do a poor job of handling conflicts. Anger in congregations is either repressed, only to resurface later in more intense aggression, or it is expressed in hostile, harmful ways that lead to alienation. Clergy can have an essential role in leading their congregations to new and lasting conflict resolution by teaching and modeling the skills needed to confront with care and communicate honestly, directly, and effectively. The self-image of the congregation as a whole will improve and the skills the parishioners learn will carry over into their relationships outside of church.

To move beyond conflict resolution to conflict prevention requires looking inside oneself. Conflict resolution addresses the external event that caused the conflict. Most people believe that they feel angry because of what someone has done. They believe the real way to resolve conflict is to stop the other person's behavior, then they will be happy. Of course, we can only control ourselves and not others, so the real solution to conflict is to prevent it by learning to conduct ourselves in difficult circumstances by changing our way of thinking. This requires using our spiritual intelligence.

Spiritual intelligence is the skills and behaviors needed to maintain a relationship with God and to assist in the search for meaning in life. Spiritual intelligence guides our moral and ethical decisions and must be developed from childhood. Churches can be intentional about creating a religious environment that encourages and fosters spiritual growth by finding what we are seeking inside, not outside. Learning how to get inside and experiencing the presence of God requires understanding the difference between rational thinking and conscious feeling. To become aware by feeling requires time, slowing down, and focusing. Spiritual intelligence is nurtured and developed by practice.

Youth in the church may particularly benefit from the character development that comes with spiritual discipline and they may experience a sense of belonging to God and the church community, as well as their own family. Clergy who work with youth can present alternatives to what they experience in their pop culture and allow them to question and explore the radical, counterculture ideas of the great spiritual leaders.

Many of the causes of PTSD are related to sexual trauma. The church needs to do much more work in the area of prevention of sexual violence by changing traditional Christian thinking about the moral right to control one's own body, and, as stated earlier, reimaging God to include only creative, empowering, collaborative images. Western Christian culture has taught that women must forfeit control over their bodies, especially in terms of reproduction, marriage, and sexuality. Christine Gudorf (1994), in her book *Body, Sex and Pleasure: Reconstructing Sexual Ethics,* attributes women's loss of "bodyright" to patriarchy:

> The absence of bodyright is clearest and most acute in the cases of children, of women, and of men who are in the military, especially when these are also racial/ethnic groups from lower economic classes. This fact supports the understanding of patriarchy as responsible for the absence of bodyright, for in full-blown patriarchies, the lives of women, children, slaves/servants and warriors are owned by the patriarchs, whose interests they serve. (pp. 162-163)

Women's bodies have been politicized by the patriarchal need for control, resulting in the constant battle for women to retain access to legal abortion. Most mainline Christian churches have resisted taking a pro-choice position, allowing individual women, not the government, to make decisions about their pregnancies. If a woman's religious beliefs prevent her from viewing abortion as a choice for terminating an unwanted pregnancy, then obviously she is free not to choose abortion. But the woman who is not religiously constrained must have the freedom to choose legal abortion. Otherwise, the government becomes the controlling force over a woman's body—an act of psychological, emotional, and spiritual violence.

Sexual, physical, psychological/emotional, and spiritual violence usually result in acute or chronic PTSD. The Christian church has an antiviolence ethic in the New Testament grounded in Jesus' Great Commandment to love your neighbor as yourself. The Christian love ethic should be adequate grounds for action to eliminate the possibility of sexual violence. Jesus' parable of the Good Samaritan is a model for intervention in response to a victim (Luke 10:29-37). Even with these strong scriptural messages, the crucifixion of Jesus still presents a theological problem for victims of violence that the church needs to take seriously and explore. For many survivors of trauma, the victimization of Jesus in the crucifixion seems to imply sanction of violence. Jesus' violent death is interpreted to be an act of salvation for all humankind. By encouraging people to pattern their lives on Jesus', women and other marginalized persons at risk for victimization are being asked to accept their suffering as virtuous rather than being empowered to call out for justice and restitution. The crucifixion has also been interpreted traditionally as God's will for his son. This has led some contemporary theologians to question what this says about God as initiating and condoning abuse of his child. Pastors who find themselves preaching on the passion and crucifixion of Jesus have a responsibility to challenge themselves to a deep reflective process before promoting a theological interpretation that could contribute to furthering the spiritual trauma of a victim of violence.

In James Newton Poling's (1991) book, *The Abuse of Power: A Theological Problem,* he devotes a chapter to several principles that he believes will lead to more effective ministry for the prevention of violence. He accurately points out that the church has silenced and isolated victims of sexual violence and must change by offering victims resources for prevention and healing. The Reverend Jackson Day, Executive Director of the National Conference of Viet Nam Veteran Ministers, is engaged in a major project called "Pastoral Care for Trauma Survivors," a training curriculum for educating clergy and their congregations how to respond to victims of trauma by following the principle of RICH: respect, information, connection, and hope. The RICH concept comes from a curriculum produced by the Sidran Foundation of Lutherville, Maryland, targeted for personnel in public mental health care.

Churches should cosponsor abuse awareness and prevention seminars and healing workshops for trauma survivors in cooperation with local mental health agencies and law enforcement personnel in an effort to create a communitywide response to domestic and sexual violence, gang violence, ritual abuse, school violence, and elder abuse. Town and city managers should work with local clergy and mental health professionals to create a trained team of local people who can respond quickly in the event of a natural disaster or traumatic event, such as a bombing or mass murder.

Churches must be willing to acknowledge the negative effects of patriarchy on women and men and teach alternative ways for men to use power that is mutual and lifegiving. Perpetrators of violence who are active, well-regarded members of a church must be held accountable for their behavior.

Churches can cosponsor programs with their local schools to help parents raise children who resist violence. Aggressive and violent behavior is often learned early in a child's life. Parents can be taught about their roles in preventing violence by providing protective and loving homes. We are not born with the knowledge it takes to be effective parents. Churches should be a nonjudgmental place for adults to admit this and seek more guidance and awareness.

Churches must be proactive in prevention of abuse in their faith community by acknowledging it can happen in churches and abuse can be perpetrated by clergy and other church leaders. Institutional policies and procedures must be in place to provide a process for investigating allegations of sexual misconduct. Priority must be given to preventing abuse and protecting victims.

Pastors have a special opportunity to prevent family violence during marriage preparation. All couples should meet with their pastor for several sessions prior to the wedding ceremony, to participate in a program designed by the pastor. With the possible assistance of laypeople, the program should stress the fundamental equality of men and women, the avoidance of gender stereotypes, and the issue of violence by stating clearly that any degree of violence is not acceptable. It is an important strategy to raise awareness about family violence by defining the different types of abuse and reflecting with the couple on their families of origin to reveal any history of witnessing of violence or victimization by a family member. Pastors should also explore authority, power, and control in the couple's relationship, how they deal with anger and conflict, and assist them in learning nonviolent methods of communication and dispute resolution.

If a person studies the history of the Christian church, he or she will learn that the church has initiated war and justified doing so as having a "holy purpose." Such a history seems a major contradiction to the message Jesus delivered about peace. The contemporary North American Christian church has taken a greater role in promoting peace and an end to war as a means of solving conflict. Peace initiatives as a preventive approach to conflict and disharmony should be promoted by the church. The church should be a place where the people are part of a movement to find ways to survive our human reactions to diversity. Pastors should be leaders in an effort to create a culture of peace in the midst of differences.

Peace, in the Hebrew biblical sense of "shalom," is more than the absence of war. It also connotes the spiritual value of justice—the seeking of balance, fairness, and caring for the concerns, rights, and privileges of all effected. After having spent time as a chaplain working with combat veterans, hearing their stories, and witnessing the long-term effects of war on the human body, the psyche, and the spirit, I am more than ever an advocate of peacemaking. I frequently wear a button on my shirt at work that reads, "Honor Our Vets—No More War." The veterans themselves have responded in an overwhelmingly positive way to this viewpoint. Peacemaking is a spiritual discipline that engages the qualities, values, ethics, and approaches in human relationships in order to build tolerance for diversity, eventually leading to affirmation of differences. Imagine what the world would be like if we committed as much money and human energy to peacemaking as we have to making war.

Epilogue

Survivors of trauma events are members of our congregations; they are people who may seek us out when struggling to make sense of a horrific incident. As clergy, we have a responsibility to respond to the spiritual crisis of survivors with respect, understanding, and as a source of support and hope. To do so, we need to have knowledge of the common manifestations and symptoms of post-traumatic stress disorder and the psychological problems that accompany the acute symptoms. We need to be aware of the causes of PTSD and what we can do to prevent further traumatic events.

The theological dimensions of trauma touch upon a survivor's spirituality and may challenge previously held religious beliefs. The pastor's response to the questions that may arise should guide the survivor toward spiritual healing. A sensitive pastor will be aware of issues of language, symbols, race, class, gender, sexuality, and culture, and be able to offer rituals of healing when appropriate. Pastoral support for those with PTSD includes alternative spiritual practices and therapies. A pastor's willingness to participate with a team of mental health care providers, doctors, and others will serve to strengthen the survivor's sense of a network of caregivers.

Working with persons with chronic PTSD while providing pastoral care to other members of one's congregations at the same time, requires that pastors be spiritually grounded themselves, engaged in supervision of their work, and seeing to it that they have a balance of work, exercise, and recreation daily. Remaining passionate and productive in pastoral ministry means having an awareness of one's limitations and protecting one's own mental health, creativity, and primary relationships. Spiritual self-care for the pastor is essential.

As church leaders, pastors are in a position to facilitate churches in their exploration of the church's role in preventing PTSD. Critiquing church policies, liturgy, language, etc., will raise consciousness about the ways the church may be complicit in its perpetuation of patriarchy and abuse of power that contribute to the causes of PTSD. Upholding the biblical mandates for compassion, forgiveness, love, peace, and justice ties into mission activities that can happen at the community level.

In many rural churches and small communities, it has been my experience that the pastors and rabbis are just beginning to give attention to the topics and issues presented in this book, having ministered under the assumption that the causes of PTSD do not exist in their quiet, sheltered towns. The reality is that all towns, regardless of size, have violence occurring in the form of domestic and sexual violence, ritual abuse, elder abuse, marital rape, rape, and harassment and bullying at school. The small town may also experience a natural disaster at any time. The challenge in small towns is the isolation that keeps many people from getting help when needed and the extreme attitudes about privacy in the home.

Clergy could benefit from discussing among themselves the topics in this book and the ways the issues pertain to their communities. Studying together and engaging in theological reflection may infuse new attitudes and practices that will expand their compassion and ability to be present with survivors and perpetrators of violence.

God calls us to walk with the wounded as living reminders of God's love; offering guidance, support, and hope for their spiritual journey to full recovery. This is soul work—heart work—and demands the best of us. May we all strive to be instruments of peace and healing until God's realm on earth is fully known.

Appendix

Spiritual Assessment

Self-Reflection Questions

Who am I?
What am I here for?
What is my path?
Why is there suffering?
Why is there evil?
Is death the end?
How can I serve God?
What gives my life meaning?
Who will love me?
How well am I able to love others?
What is wrong with me?
Where is God?

Clergy/Chaplain Interview Questions

Do you identify with a particular religion or denomination?
Do you attend worship?
Did you have religious education as a child?
Do you believe in God or a higher power?
Do you nurture your relationship with God by the use of spiritual practices such as: prayer, meditation, Yoga, Bible reading, reading of other sacred Scripture, a twelve-step program, devotional reading, mission projects, fasting, music, etc.?
What does your relationship with God mean to you?
Are you experiencing any sense of alienation in your relationship with God? With family? With friends?
What gives your life meaning? Hope?
Who or what do you turn to in times of trouble?
How have you coped with stress?

Did you serve in the military? Were you in combat?

How is your current situation affecting your relationship with God?

Is there a loss of purpose or direction?

Is there a sense of overwhelming guilt?

Do you feel your suffering is punishment for your actions?

Can you describe any positive spiritual experiences?

How is your quality of life at this time?

What are your current spiritual needs? What can I do to help you meet those needs?

Are your health problems affecting your relationship with God?

Bibliography

American Academy of Pediatrics. *Raising Children to Resist Violence: What You Can Do.* Elk Grove, IL: Author, 1996.

American Psychiatric Association (APA). *Diagnostic and Statistical Manual of Mental Disorder, Fourth Edition, Text Revision.* Washington, DC: American Psychiatric Association, 2000.

American Psychological Association. *Post-Traumatic Stress Disorder (PTSD).* On-line public information: <http://www.apa.org>.

Anderson, Sherry Ruth and Patricia Hopkins. *The Feminine Face of God: The Unfolding of the Sacred in Women.* New York: Bantam Books, 1991.

Augsberger, David. *Caring Enough to Forgive.* Ventura: Regal Books, 1981.

Barton, Gail M. and Lawrence L. LaPierre. "The Spiritual Sequelae of Combat as Reflected by Vietnam Veterans Suffering from PTSD." *American Journal of Pastoral Counseling,* 2(3) (1999): 3-21.

Bass, Ellen and Laura Davis. *The Courage to Heal.* New York: Harper Perennial Library, 1988.

Bergen, Raquel K. *Marital Rape.* Online document: <http//www.vaw.umn.edu/Vawnet/mrape.htm>. (March 1999): 1-12.

Blair, D. Thomas and Nancy A. Hildreth. "PTSD and the Vietnam Veteran: The Battle for Treatment." *Journal of Psychosocial Nursing,* 29(10) (1991): 15-20.

Bloomquist, Karen L. "Sexual Violence: Patriarchy's Offense and Defense." In Joanne Carlson Brown and Carole R. Bohn, eds. *Christianity, Patriarchy, and Abuse: A Feminist Critique* (pp. 62-69). New York: The Pilgrim Press, 1989.

Blume, E. Sue. *Secret Survivors: Uncovering Incest and Its Aftereffects in Women.* New York: John Wiley and Sons, 1990.

Boston Women's Health Book Collective. *The New Our Bodies, Ourselves.* New York: Simon & Schuster, 1984.

Brown, Joanne Carlson and Carole R. Bohn, eds. *Christianity, Patriarchy, and Abuse: A Feminist Critique.* New York: The Pilgrim Press, 1989.

Brown, Robert McAfee. *Religion and Violence.* Stanford: The Portable Stanford, 1973.

Brownmiller, Susan. *Against Our Wills: Men, Women, and Rape.* New York: Simon & Schuster, 1975.

Bussart, J. M. K. *Battered Women: From a Theology of Suffering to an Ethic of Empowerment.* New York: Division for Mission in North America, Lutheran Church in America, 1986.

Clergy Development Conference. *Bearing Fruit: A Resource for Clergy Self-Assessment.* New York: The Cornerstone Project, 1992.

Clinebell, Howard. *Basic Types of Pastoral Care and Counseling: Resources for the Ministry of Healing and Growth,* Revised Edition. Nashville: Abingdon Press, 1984.

Coffey, Rebecca. *Unspeakable Truths and Happy Endings: Human Cruelty and the New Trauma Therapy.* Lutherville, MD: The Sidran Press, 1998.

Davis, Laura. *Allies in Healing.* San Francisco: Harper Perennial, 1991.

Dean, Donna M. *Warriors Without Weapons: The Victimization of Military Women.* Pasadena, CA: Menerva Center, 1997.

Doehring, Carrie. *Taking Care: Monitoring Power Dynamics and Relational Boundaries in Pastoral Care and Counseling.* Nashville: Abingdon Press, 1995.

Dossey, Larry. *Healing Words: The Power of Prayer and the Practice of Medicine.* San Francisco: Harper, 1993.

Drake, Katherine. "Our Flying Nightingales in Vietnam." *Reader's Digest,* December 1967: 75.

Ellwood, Garcia Fay. *Batter My Heart.* Wallingford, CT: Pendle Hill Publications (#282), 1988.

Enright, R.D. and J. North, eds. *Exploring Forgiveness.* Madison: University of Wisconsin Press, 1998.

Farmer, Steven. *Adult Children of Abusive Parents: A Healing Program for Those Who Have Been Physically, Sexually, or Emotionally Abused.* New York: Ballantine Books, 1989.

Flannery, Raymond. *Post-Traumatic Stress Disorder: The Victim's Guide to Healing and Recovery.* New York: Crossroads Publishing Company, 1995.

Fortune, Marie Marshall. *Sexual Violence: The Unmentionable Sin: An Ethical and Pastoral Perspective.* New York: The Pilgrim Press, 1983.

_____. *Keeping the Faith: Guidance for Christian Women Facing Abuse.* San Francisco: Harper, 1987.

_____. *Is Nothing Sacred? When Sex Invades the Pastoral Relationship.* San Francisco: Harper & Row, 1989.

_____. *Violence in the Family—A Workshop Curriculum for Clergy and Other Helpers.* Cleveland: The Pilgrim Press, 1991.

_____. *Love Does No Harm: Sexual Ethics for the Rest of Us.* New York: Continuum, 1995.

_____. *Broken Vows: Religious Perspectives on Domestic Violence* [video]. Seattle, WA: Center for the Prevention of Sexual and Domestic Violence.

Fox, Matthew. *A Spirituality Named Compassion.* San Francisco: Harper, 1979.

Furey, Joan A. "Women Vietnam Veterans: A Comparison of Studies." *Journal of Psychosocial Nursing,* 29(3) (1991): 11-13.

Garrison, Louise M. "Where Was God?" in *Sojourners,* 13(6) (November/December 1984): 23-24.

Goleman, Daniel. *Emotional Intelligence: Why It Can Matter More Than IQ.* New York: Bantam Books, 1995.

Goodwin, Jim. *Readjustment Problems Among Vietnam Veterans.* Cincinnati: Disabled American Veterans, 1981.

Gottlieb, Lynn. *She Who Dwells Within: A Feminist Vision of Renewed Judaism.* San Francisco: Harper, 1995.

Greven, Philip. *Spare the Child: The Religious Roots of Punishment and the Psychological Impact of Physical Abuse.* New York: Alfred A. Knopf, 1991.

Grollman, Earl A. *Suicide: Prevention, Intervention, Postvention.* Boston: Beacon Press, 1988.

Gudorf, Christine. *Body, Sex, and Pleasure: Reconstructing Sexual Ethics.* Cleveland: Pilgrim Press, 1994.

Harrison, Beverly and Carol S. Robb, eds. *Making the Connections: Essays in Feminist Social Ethics.* Boston: Beacon Press, 1985.

Herman, Judith Lewis. *Trauma and Recovery.* New York: Basic Books, 1992.

Heyward, Carter. *When Boundaries Betray Us: Beyond Illusions of What Is Ethical in Therapy and Life.* San Francisco: Harper, 1993.

Hill, E. Wayne and Paul Mullen. "Contexts for Understanding Forgiveness and Repentance as Discovery: A Pastoral Care Perspective." *The Journal of Pastoral Care,* 54(3) (Fall 2000): 287-296.

Holm, Jeanne. *Women in the Military: An Unfinished Revolution,* Revised Edition. Novato: Presidio, 1992.

Holy Bible. New International Version. East Brunswick, NJ: International Bible Society, 1984.

Holy Bible. New Revised Standard Version. New York: New Oxford Press, 1991.

Horowitz, M.J. and G.F. Soloman. "Prediction of delayed stress response syndrome in Vietnam veterans." *Journal of Social Issues: Soldiers In and After Vietnam,* 31(4) (1975): 67-80.

Imbens, Annie and Jonker Ineke. *Christianity and Incest.* Minneapolis: Fortress Press, 1992.

Jack, Dana Crowley. *Silencing the Self: Women and Depression.* New York: Harper Perennial, 1991.

Johnson, David and Jeff VanVonderen. *The Subtle Power of Spiritual Abuse: Recognizing and Escaping Spiritual Manipulation and False Spiritual Authority Within the Church.* Minneapolis: Bethany House Publishers, 1991.

Jones, F.D. and A.W. Johnson. "Medical psychiatric treatment policy and practice in Vietnam." *Journal of Social Issues: Soldiers In and After Vietnam,* 31(4) (1975): 49-65.

Kelsey, Morton. *Psychology, Medicine and Christian Healing.* San Francisco: Harper & Row, 1988.

Kennedy, Dan. "Coping with Loss: Teachings of a Master." In *World,* 14(4) (July/August, 2000): 17-19.

Kessler, R., A. Sonnega, E. Bromet, J. Hughes, and C.B. Nelson. "Post-traumatic stress disorder in the National Comorbidity Survey." *Archives of General Psychiatry*, 52 (1995): 1048-1060.

Kornfeld, Margaret. *Cultivating Wholeness*. New York: Continuum, 1998.

Kübler-Ross, Elisabeth. *On Death and Dying*. New York: Macmillan Publishing Co. Inc., 1969.

Kuenning, Delores A. *Life After Vietnam: How Veterans and Their Loved Ones Heal the Psychological Wounds of War*. New York: Paragon House, 1991.

Kulka, R.A., W.E. Schlenger, J.A. Fairbank, R. Hough, B.K. Jordan, C.R. Marmar, and D. Weiss. "The National Vietnam Veterans Readjustment Study (NVVRS): Contractual report of findings." In *Trauma and the Vietnam War Generation*. New York: Brunner/Mazel, 1990.

Kushner, Harold. *When Bad Things Happen to Good People*. New York: Shocken Books, 1981.

_____. *How Good Do We Have to Be? A New Understanding of Guilt and Forgiveness*. Arlington: Little, Brown and Co., 1996.

Lebacqz, Karen. *Professional Ethics: Power and Paradox*. Nashville: Abingdon, 1985.

Lee, Mary Price and Lee Richards. *Everything You Need to Know About Natural Disasters and Post-Traumatic Stress Disorder*. New York: The Rosen Publishing Group, 1996.

Levine, Peter A. *Waking the Tiger: Healing Trauma*. Berkeley: North Atlantic Books, 1997.

Lew, Mike. *Victims No Longer: Men Recovering from Incest and Other Sexual Child Abuse*. New York: Harper & Row, Perennial Library, 1990.

Matsakis, Aphrodite. *Post Traumatic Stress Disorder: A Complete Treatment Guide*. Oakland: New Harbinger Publications, 1994.

_____. *Trust After Trauma: A Guide to Relationships for Survivors and Those Who Love Them*. Oakland, CA: New Harbinger Publications, 1998.

McFague, Sallie. *Models of God: Theology for an Ecological, Nuclear Age*. Philadelphia: Fortress Press, 1987.

McGoldrick, Monica, ed. *Re-Visioning Family Therapy: Race, Culture, and Gender in Clinical Practice*. New York: The Guilford Press, 1998.

McKay, Matthew, Peter D. Rogers, and Judith McKay. *When Anger Hurts: Quieting the Storm Within*. Oakland, CA: New Harbinger Publications, 1989.

Miller, Alice. *For Your Own Good: Hidden Cruelty in Child-Rearing and the Roots of Violence*. New York: Farrar, Straus, Giroux, 1983.

_____. *Thou Shalt Not Be Aware: Society's Betrayal of the Child*. New York: New American Library, 1984.

Miller, Dusty. *Women Who Hurt Themselves: A Book of Hope and Understanding*. New York: BasicBooks, 1994.

Miller, Melissa. *Family Violence: The Compassionate Church Response*. Waterloo, Ontario: Herald Press, 1994.

Moessner, Jeanne Stevenson, ed. *The Handbook of Womencare: Through the Eyes of Women*. Minneapolis: Fortress Press, 1996.

Muller, Wayne. *Legacy of the Heart: The Spiritual Advantages of a Painful Childhood*. New York: Simon & Schuster, 1992.

National Crime Victimization Survey, Bureau of Justice Statistics, U.S. Department of Justice, 1997.

Nelson, James B. *Between Two Gardens: Reflections on Sexuality and Religious Experience*. New York: The Pilgrim Press, 1983.

_____. *Intimate Connection: Male Sexuality, Masculine Spirituality*. Philadelphia: The Westminster Press, 1988.

Neuger, Christie Cozad, ed. *The Arts of Ministry: Feminist-Womanist Approaches*. Louisville, KY: Westminster John Knox Press, 1996.

Oates, Wayne E. *Pastoral Care and Counseling in Grief and Separation*. Philadelphia: Fortress, 1976.

_____. *Pastoral Counseling*. Louisville: Westminster John Knox Press. 1982.

Pellauer, Mary D., Barbara Chester, and Jane Boyajian. *Sexual Assault and Abuse: A Handbook for Clergy and Religious Professionals*. San Francisco: Harper, 1991.

Plaskow, Judith. *Standing Again at Sinai*. San Francisco: Harper, 1990.

Poling, James Newton. *The Abuse of Power: A Theological Problem*. Nashville: Abingdon Press, 1991.

Ragsdale, Katherine Hancock, ed. *Boundary Wars: Intimacy and Distance in Healing Relationships*. Cleveland: Pilgrim Press, 1996.

Rediger, Lloyd G. *Ministry & Sexuality: Cases, Counseling, and Care*. Minneapolis: Augsburg Fortress Press, 1990.

Reilly, Patricia Lynn. *A God Who Looks Like Me: Discovering a Woman-Affirming Spirituality*. New York: Ballantine, 1995.

Rienstra, Marchieve Vroon. *Swallow's Nest: A Feminine Reading of the Psalms*. New York: Friendship Press, 1992.

Rosenbeck, Robert. *Advances in the Care of Post-Traumatic Stress Disorder* [video]. West Haven, CT: Evaluation Division, VA National Center for PTSD, 1997.

Siemon-Netto, U. *The Acquittal of God—A Theology for Vietnam Veterans*. New York: The Pilgrim Press, 1990.

Silverstein, Shel. *The Missing Piece*. San Francisco: HarperCollins, 1976.

Snorton, Teresa E. "The Legacy of the African-American Matriarch: New Perspectives for Pastoral Care." In Jeanne Stevenson Moessner, ed., *Christianity Through the Eyes of Women: The Handbook of Womencare* (pp. 50-65). Minneapolis: Augsburg Fortress, 1996.

Solomon, S.D. and J.R.T. Davidson. "Trauma: Prevalence, impairment, service use, and cost," *Journal of Clinical Psychiatry* 58 (suppl 9) (1997): 5-11.

Starhawk. *Truth or Dare: Encounters with Power, Authority, and Mystery*. San Francisco: Harper and Row, 1987.

Stone, Howard W. *Crisis Counseling.* Philadelphia: Fortress Press, 1976.

Tobias, Madeleine Landau and Janja Lalich. *Captive Hearts, Captive Minds: Freedom and Recovery from Cults and Other Abusive Relationships.* Almeda, CA: Hunter House, 1994.

Trible, Phyllis. *God and Rhetoric of Sexuality.* San Francisco: Harper, 1978.

VanDevanter, Lynda and Joan A. Furey, eds. *Visions of War, Dreams of Peace: Writings of Women in the Vietnam War.* New York: Warner Books, 1991.

Wachtel, Ted. *Real Justice.* Pipersville, PA: The Piper's Press, 1997.

Walch, Mimi Doe. *10 Principles for Spiritual Parenting: Nurturing Your Child's Soul.* New York: Harper Perennial Library, 1998.

Wallis, Jim. *The Soul of Politics.* New York: The New Press and Orbis Books, 1994.

Ward, Hanna and Jennifer Wild, eds. *Human Rites: Worship Resources for an Age of Change.* London: Mowbray, 1995.

Williams, James G. *The Bible, Violence & the Sacred: Liberation from the Myth of Sanctioned Violence.* San Francisco: Harper, 1991.

Williamson, Cris. "Song of the Soul." On *The Changer and the Changed,* audiocassette, Bird Ankles Music, 1975.

Wuellner, Flora Slosson. *Prayer, Stress, & Our Inner Wounds.* Nashville: The Upper Room, 1985.

Yehuda, Rachel, ed. *Psychological Trauma.* Washington, DC: American Psychiatric Press, Inc., 1998.

Web Sites

American Academy of Experts in Traumatic Stress: <http://www.aaets.org>

American Psychological Association: <http://www.apa.org>

Carl T. Hayden Veterans Affairs Medical Center: <http://www.phoenix.med.va.gov/HealthSvcs/pts_resources.htm>

Center for Women Veterans: <http://www.womenvets.com>

Child Trauma Home Page: <http://www.childtrauma.com/>

CIVITAS Child Trauma Programs: <http://public.bcm.tmc.edu>

Forgiveness Therapy: <http://www.forgiver.net>

Mental Health Net: <http://www.mentalhelp.net>

Mental Help Net: <http://mentalhelp.net/poc/view_links.php/It/Information/cn/Trauma>

National Center for Police Officers with PTSD: <http://www.ncpoptsd.freeyello.com/>

National Center for Post-Traumatic Stress Disorder: <http://www.dartmouth.edu/dms/ptsd>, or <http://www.ncptsd.org/>

National Center for Victims of Crime: <http://www.ncvc.org/>

National Conference of Viet Nam Veteran Ministers: <http://www.vietnamveteranministers.org>

National Victim Center: <http://www.ncvc.org/>

Sidran Foundation: <http://www.sidran.org/>
The National Coalition of Homicide Survivors, Inc.: <http://www.mivictims.org/nchs/>
This Healing Journey: <http://welcome.to/ThisHealingJourney2>
Trauma Central: <http://home.earthlink.net/~hopefull/>

Index

Abortion, 100
Abuse of Power: A Theological Problem (Poling), 101
Abusive relationships, 59
Acceptance, 22
Alcoholics Anonymous, 27, 38, 85
Alienation from God, 46, 53
Amphetamines, 44
Anger
  assigned, 37
  between couples, 102
  empowerment, 37
  at God, 21, 36
  holding onto, 39
  outbursts, 14, 18
  power of, 37
  regulation of, 18
  repressing, 18
  sanctioned by God, 23
  self-directed, 8
  spiritual nature of, 23, 24
  toward offender, 11
  toward self, 21
  toward survivor, 11
Anorexic starvation, 27
Anxiety, 18, 38, 77, 80

Bargaining, 21
"Bearing Fruit," 102. *See also* Clergy, self-assessment
Benzedrine, 45
Blame, 21, 31, 52, 61
Blume, E. Sue, 25
Body, Sex and Pleasure (Gudorf), 100
Boundary issues, 6, 9, 89, 91. *See also* Pastor
Boundary Wars: Intimacy and Distance in Healing Relationships (Ragsdale), 91
Bulimic bingeing, 27

Center for Women Veterans, 50-51
Character development, 99
Christianity, Patriarchy, and Abuse (Brown, Bohn eds.), 97
Class issues, 61, 62-63
Clergy
  burnout, 90, 92
  centered in God, 92
  clergywomen, 33
  disconnection, 92
  ethical behavior, 91
  misconduct, 6
  self-assessment, 92-93
  self-care, 89-93
  self-nurture, 91
  self-respect, 92
  supervision, 66, 90
  use of power, 98
Community, 28, 36
Compassion, 35, 57, 58
Conflict resolution and prevention, 99
"Contexts for Understanding Forgiveness and Repentance as Discovery" (Hill, Mullen), 38
Continuing education, 84
Cornerstone Project, 92
Counseling, 90-92
  brief, 81
  spiritual, 81, 85
The Courage to Heal (Bass, Davis), 70
Crisis Counseling (Stone), 66
Crisis intervention, 66, 83, 85
Cult abuse, 4
Cultivating Wholeness (Kornfeld), 28

Denial, 20
Depression, 8, 20-21, 32, 52-53
Diagnostic and Statistical Manual of Mental Disorders (DSM-IV-TR), 1, 13-15

117

Domestic violence, 2, 6, 7, 51
DSM-III, 43

EKP (emotional kinesthetic
    psychotherapy), 48
EMDR (eye movement desensitization
    and reprocessing), 48
Episcopal Church Foundation, 92
Evil. *See* Theological dimensions
Eyewitness to violence
    children as, 10
    pastoral support for, 10-11
    rescue teams as, 10

Faith statements, 63
Feminist liberation theology, 53
Flashbacks, 18
Forgiveness, 9, 31, 53, 80. *See also* God
    and grief work, 38
    and healing, 38-40
    and reconciliation, 38, 39
    stages of, 38

Gender issues, 51-53, 59-61
Genital mutilation, 4
    medical consequences, 5
God
    alienation from, 8, 9, 46
    alternative images of, 53, 82
    anger at, 21
    blaming of, 31
    as cause of illness, 56
    as covenantal companion, 33
    discipling by, 32
    exercises justice, 32
    faithfulness of, 79
    the Father, 81
    forgiveness, 79
    as healer, 56, 79
    as initiator of suffering, 32
    justice of, 32, 33, 78
    loss of faith in, 19
    loyal, 79
    merciful, 81
    mercy of, 45, 78
    names for, 82

God *(continued)*
    omnipotent, 32
    power of, 11
    presence of, 38
    punishing, 31, 32
    role in suffering, 32
    spirit of, 87
    steadfast love of, 11, 79, 95
    testing faith, 35
    violent, 78
Grief, 18-23, 38
    acceptance, 22
    associated medical problems, 18
    counseling, 65
    incomplete, 18
    stages, 19, 20
    unresolved, 19
Grieving process, 22
Grollman, Rabbi Earl A., 10, 64
Guerrilla warfare, 50
Guilt
    exacerbation of, 77
    feelings of, 79
    and responsibility, 64
    and sexual orientation, 61
    and spiritual life, 45

Healing
    alternative, 85
    in Christian scriptures, 56
    communion and. *See* Liturgy
    in community, 36
    environment, 58-59
    Native American, 42
    process, 35
    rituals, 67
    spiritual, 35-42, 81, 87
    theology of, 56
    and vulnerability, 62
    workshops, 101
Holotropic breathwork, 40, 41-42
Hope
    as antidote for despair, 99
    in the future, 19
    source of, 46
    spiritual nature of, 31
*Human Rites: Worship Resources for an
        Age of Change* (Ward, Wild), 67
Hypervigilance, 14, 17

Incest, 4
Incident reduction treatment, 48
Intimacy, 7, 19, 91-92
Is Nothing Sacred? (Fortune), 6

Job. *See* Scripture

Lamentations. *See* Scripture
Language, 67
Listening skills, 58, 84
Liturgy
  communion and healing, 67-85
  ritual, 67
Loss, 19-20
Love ethic, 100

Marijuana, 44
Maternalism, 63
Matsakis, Aphrodite, 19-20
Meditation, 40-41
Multiculturalism, 61
Music therapy, 40-41

National Conference of Viet Nam
    Veteran Ministers, 101
National Crime Victimization Survey, 3
National Vietnam Veterans
    Readjustment Study
    (NVVRS), 49
The New Our Bodies, Ourselves
    (Boston Women's Health
    Collective), 4, 5
Nurses, 50

On Death and Dying (Kübler-Ross), 20
Operation Desert Storm, 48, 51

Parentification, 38
Partnership model, 58, 91, 98

Pastor. *See also* Clergy
  boundaries, 55, 92
  boundary issues, 6
  co-dependent, 27
  companion, 36
  complications, 57
  disconnection, 92
  displaced anger, 37
  ecclesiastical power, 98
  education of, 55
  and health care team, 83
  neglect of family, 90
  as observer, 58
  parish-pastor relations, 91
  passionate ministry of, 92
  professional certification of, 83
  professional identity, 91
  role of, 29, 55
  self-care, 89-93
  setting limits of, 90
  spiritual growth of, 98
  as spiritual guides, 37, 46
  support group for, 90
  theology of, 55
Pastoral care
  with African-American women, 62
  and confidentiality, 91
  documentation of, 85
  limitations of, 55
  making referrals, 55, 83, 85, 86
  presence and detachment, 58-59
  privileged communication, 84
  skills, 55
  supervision of, 66, 90
"Pastoral Care for Trauma Survivors,"
    101
Paternalism, 63
Patriarchal culture, 60
Patriarchy
  definition, 96-97
  dismantling, 97-98
  early church and, 98
  loss of "body-right" and, 100
  negative effects of, 102
  system of, 51
Patronizing, 57
Peace, 29, 39, 103
Perpetrator, 60-61, 79, 80
Phenothiazines, 44
Polarity therapy, 40-41

Post-traumatic stress disorder
  causes, 1-2
  characteristics, 1
  common manifestations, 15
  definition, 1
  diagnostic criteria, 13
  new category, 43
  new treatment, 48
  prolonged, 47
  psychological complications
    addictions, 27
    anorexia, 27
    avoidance, 14
    bulimia, 27
    comorbidities, 25, 44, 47
    dissociation, 13, 25
    flashbacks, 13, 25, 26-27
    hallucinations, 13
    hypervigilance, 14, 17
    increased arousal, 14
    illusions, 13
    obsessive-compulsive disorder, 25
    outcomes, 27
    panic disorder, 25
    prevention, 95
      and biblical love ethic, 100
      by maintenance of justice, 100
    reexperiencing, 13
    splitting, 25
    symptoms, 1, 13
  theological basis of, 102
  treatment, 49
Power, 96, 98
"The Power of Anger in the Work of Love," 37
Powerlessness, 20
Prayer, 58, 76
  contemplative, 40-41
  and letting go, 40
  for survivor, 36
Presence and detachment, 58-59
Prevention
  church's role, 96, 98-103
  conflict resolution and, 99
  political issue, 98
  seminars, 101
  spiritual issue, 99
Projection, 56-57, 84

Protestant orthodoxy, 32
Psalms, 32. *See also* Scripture
Psychological pain, 25
Purity codes, 81

Racial stereotypes, 61
Racism, 61
Rage, 18
Real Justice, 40
Reconciliation, 28, 39, 77
Recovery, 15, 27-28
  groups, 85
Referrals, 55, 85-86
Reiki, 40
Restitution, 40, 101
Restorative justice, 40
Revenge, 37
Ritual abuse, 4, 34, 68

Safe touch, and healing process, 6
Scripture
  Christian, 80
  1 Corinthians, 97
  Deuteronomy, 56, 79, 95
  Ephesians, 97
  Exodus, 56, 81
  Ezekiel, 78
  Genesis, 96
  Hebrew, 77, 81, 95
  Hosea, 56, 78, 81
  Isaiah, 56, 78, 79, 81
  Jeremiah, 56
  Job, 32, 56, 78
  Judges, 78
  2 Kings, 56
  Lamentations, 32
  Leviticus, 56
  Luke, 80, 82, 101
  Malachi, 79
  Mark, 95
  Matthew, 80, 82, 89
  Micah, 79, 95
  Numbers, 56
  portrayal of God in, 56
  Psalms, 32, 56, 78, 79
  Romans, 81
  Sirach, 81
  1 Timothy, 97

Sexual harassment, 50
Sexual intimacy, 19
Sexual orientation, 61
Sexual trauma, 3-5. *See also* Trauma
Sexuality, 60, 61
Shame
 feelings of, 32, 61
 issues of, 86
 pain of, 38
 processing, 60
 rape and, 51
 unclean, 81
She Who Dwells Within: A Feminist
 *Vision of Renewed Judais*m
 (Gottlieb), 67
Sidran Foundation, 101
Sin, 57, 97, 98
Sleep disturbance, 17
Spiritual
 assessment, 84, 107-108
 autobiography, 53
 counseling, 84
 discipline, 99, 103
 growth, 98
 healing, 40, 77, 82
 intelligence, 99
 issues, 18-24, 31-33, 46
 loss, 45
 nature, 31
 needs, 81, 94
 suffering, 18
 trauma, 8-9, 44. *See also* Trauma
Spirituality
 alternative, 63-64
 compassion and, 35, 58, 96
 Celtic, 63
 definition, 1
 Druid, 63
 earth-centered, 63
 gender issues and, 51-53
 Native American, 42, 63
 Wiccan, 63
 woman-affirming, 53
Startle response, 14, 18
Stockholm syndrome, 7, 8
Stressors, 50
Suicide, 32, 50, 64-66
Survival, 17
Survivors
 counseling, 10-11

Survivors *(continued)*
 retraumatized, 32
 survivor guilt, 10
Swallow's Nest (Rienstra, Marchieve
 Vroon), 70

Theological dimensions
 commandments, 38
 crucifixion, 33, 35, 101
 deliverance, 78
 divine justice, 32, 78, 101
 evil
 allowed by God, 32
 eradication of, 35
 participating in, 45
 resistance to, 37
 theological issue, 53, 56
 incarnational, 35
 love, 37, 78, 79, 100
 mercy, 44, 78
 moral ethic, 37
 omnipotent God, 32
 power, 11, 37, 93
 punishing, 31, 32, 34, 56
 redemption, 28-29, 33, 35, 78
 repentance, 80
 restoration, 28-29, 40, 82
 resurrection, 33, 68
 salvation, 56, 101
 suffering
 alleviating, 32, 37
 of the faithful, 32
 God's will, 56, 79
 imitation of Christ, 33
 meaning of, 11
 reflection on, 56
 righteous, 78
 source of, 31
 without meaning, 9
 yielding to, 19
 theodicy, 31-33, 35, 53
Therapy
 emotional kinesthetic
 psychotherapy, 48
 holotropic breathwork, 40, 41-42
 incident reduction, 48
 massage, 41
 music, 40-41
 new approaches, 48

Therapy *(continued)*
  polarity therapy, 40-41
  Reiki, 40
  thought-field therapy, 48
Transference, 56-57, 84
Trauma
  combat, 5
  cycle of battering, 78
  domestic violence, 59, 79-80, 97,
      101
  physical trauma, 5-6, 43, 59
  psychological trauma, 7-8, 38, 43.
      See also Stockholm syndrome
  sexual trauma
    clergy sexual abuse, 9
    female circumcision, 4-5
    genital mutilation, 4-5
    incest, 4, 25, 33
    infibulation, 5
    marital rape, 3-4, 59
    molestation, 6
    rape, 50
  spiritual trauma, 8-9, 31, 43
  torture, 5
  witness to, 2
Trauma and Recovery (Herman), 2
Traumatic events, 2
Triggers, 18
Trust, 19, 46, 48, 57, 86
Truth or Dare (Starhawk), 67
The Twelve Steps, 27

Veterans
  combat, 43
  grieving process, 46-47
  Korea, 43
  Operation Desert Storm, 48
  pastoral care with, 46
  psychological breakdown, 43
  special needs, 43
  spiritual questions, 47
  stressors, 50-51
  Tet Offensive, 45
  trust issues, 48
  Vet centers, 47
  Vietnam, 49-53
  women, 49-53
  Women in the Military (Holm), 49
Victim's family, 15
Victims No Longer (Lew), 60
Violence prevention, 95, 98

When Anger Hurts (McKay, Rogers,
      and McKay), 23
*When Bad Things Happen to Good
      People* (Kushner), 36
"Where Was God?," 33
Women's bodies, 100
World (Unitarian Universalist
      Association), 10

Yoga, 6
Youth, 99-100